THROUGH MY GLASS EYE

The Photography of

ALAN KING

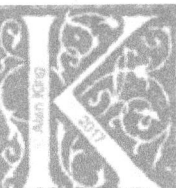

All images © Alan King 2017

Back cover photograph – thanks to Linda King

This one is for my favourite Photographers, which at the last count included anyone who picks up a camera, or a phone, and captures a moment in time

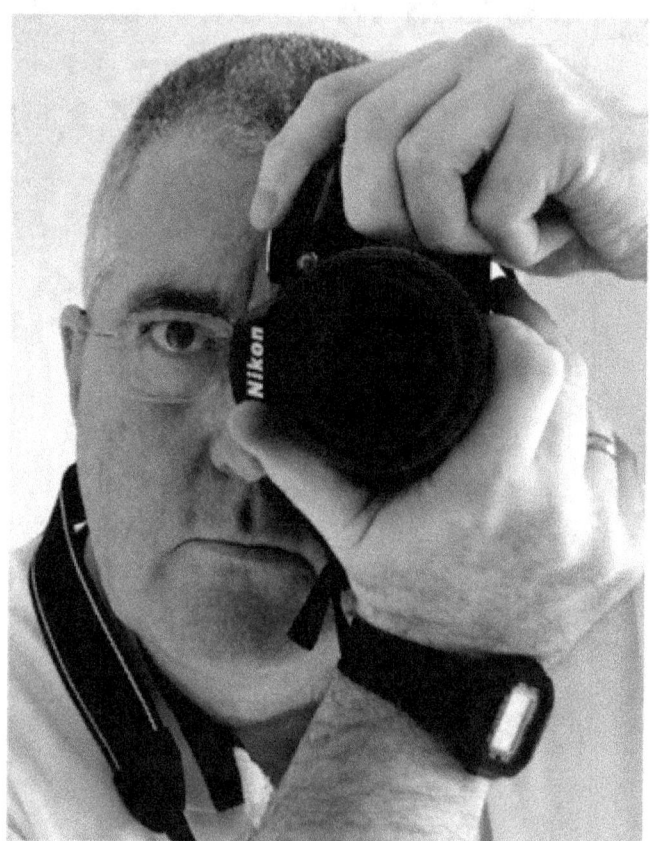

But special mention must go to Vivian Maier, Annie Leibovitz, David Bailey and Angus McBean – all a great influence

For the techies: Most of the images have been taken with my trusty N kon D3200. Old ones would have been with my 35mm Zenit E, 35mm Zenit TTL or Olympus compact Digital

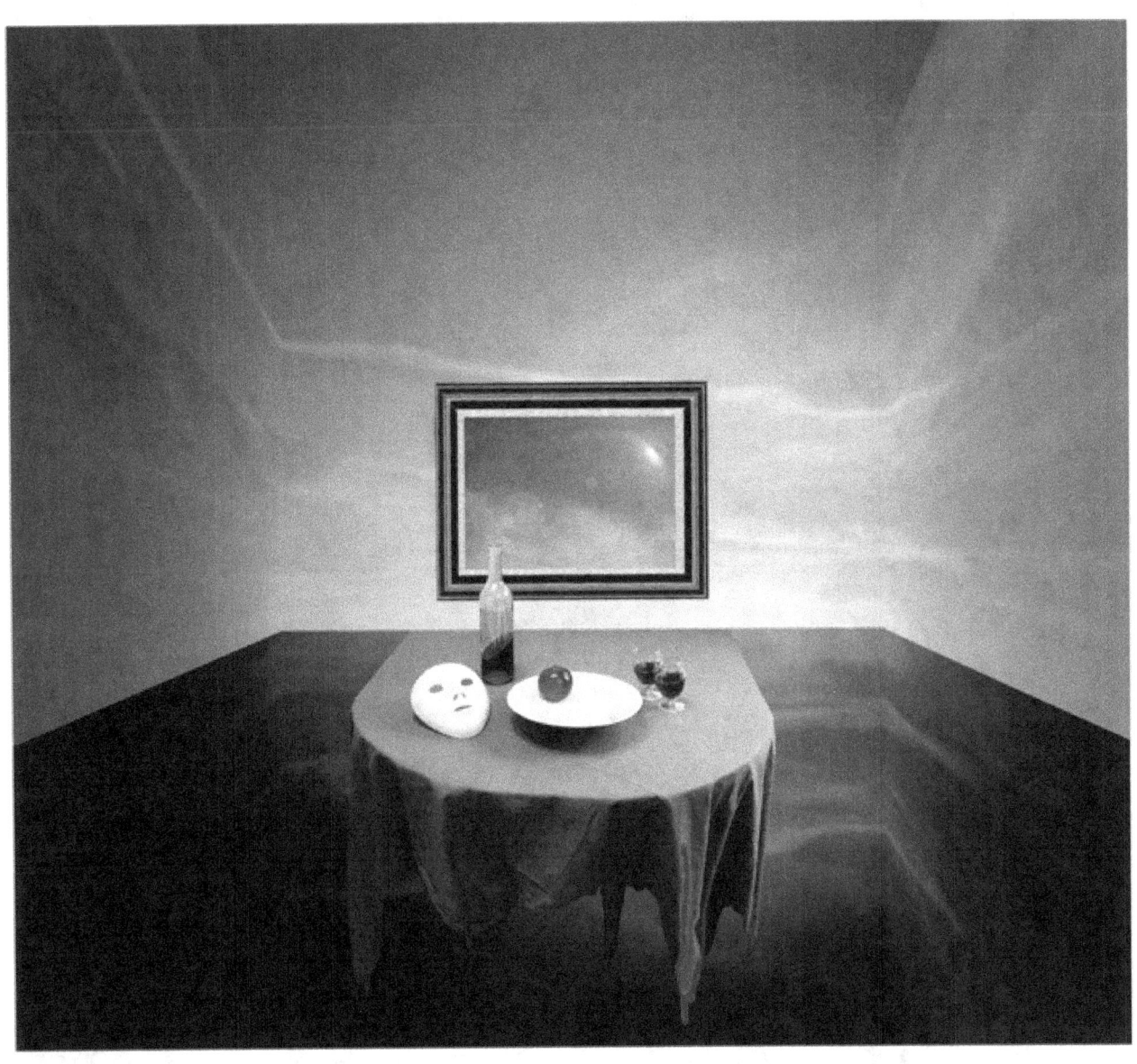

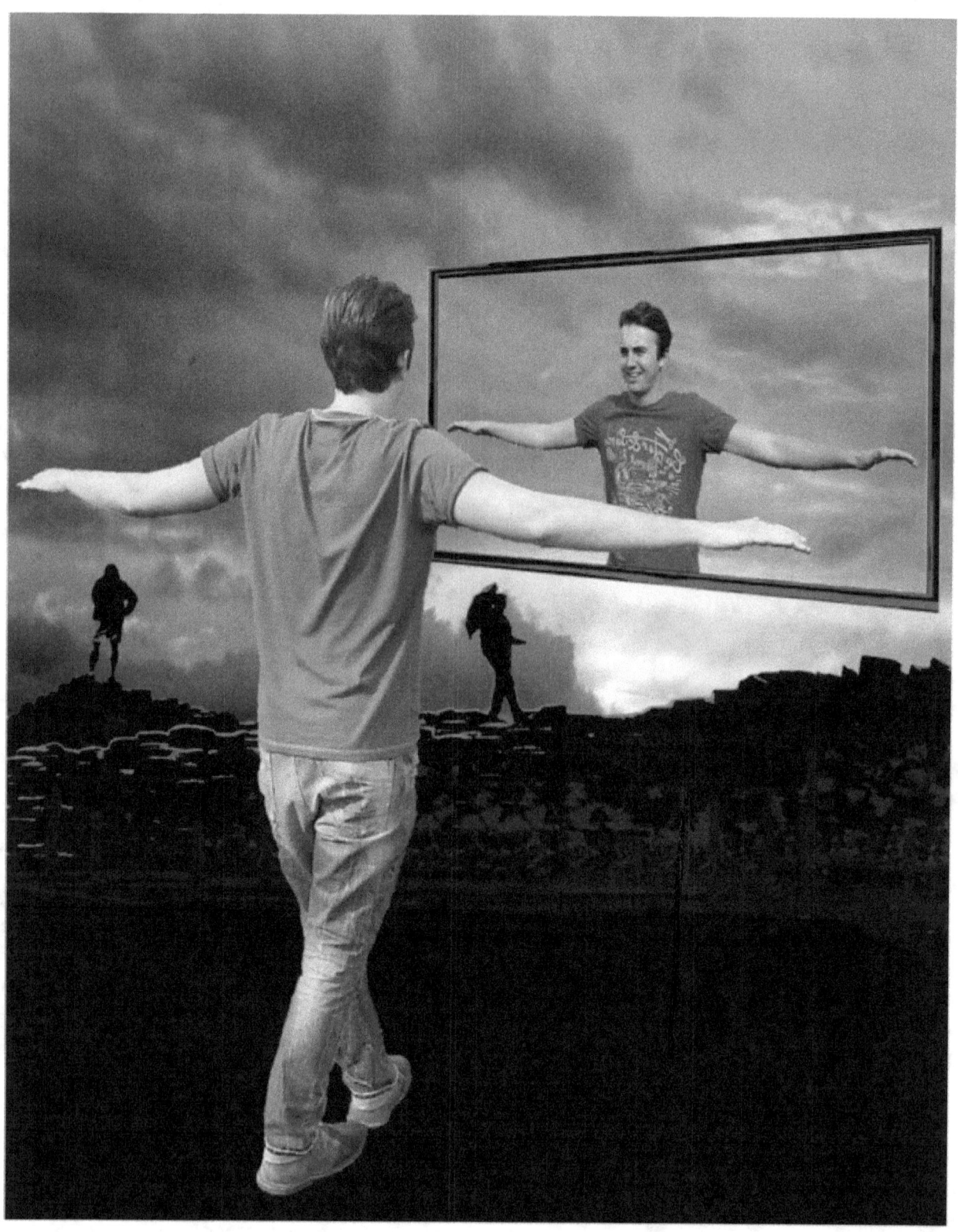

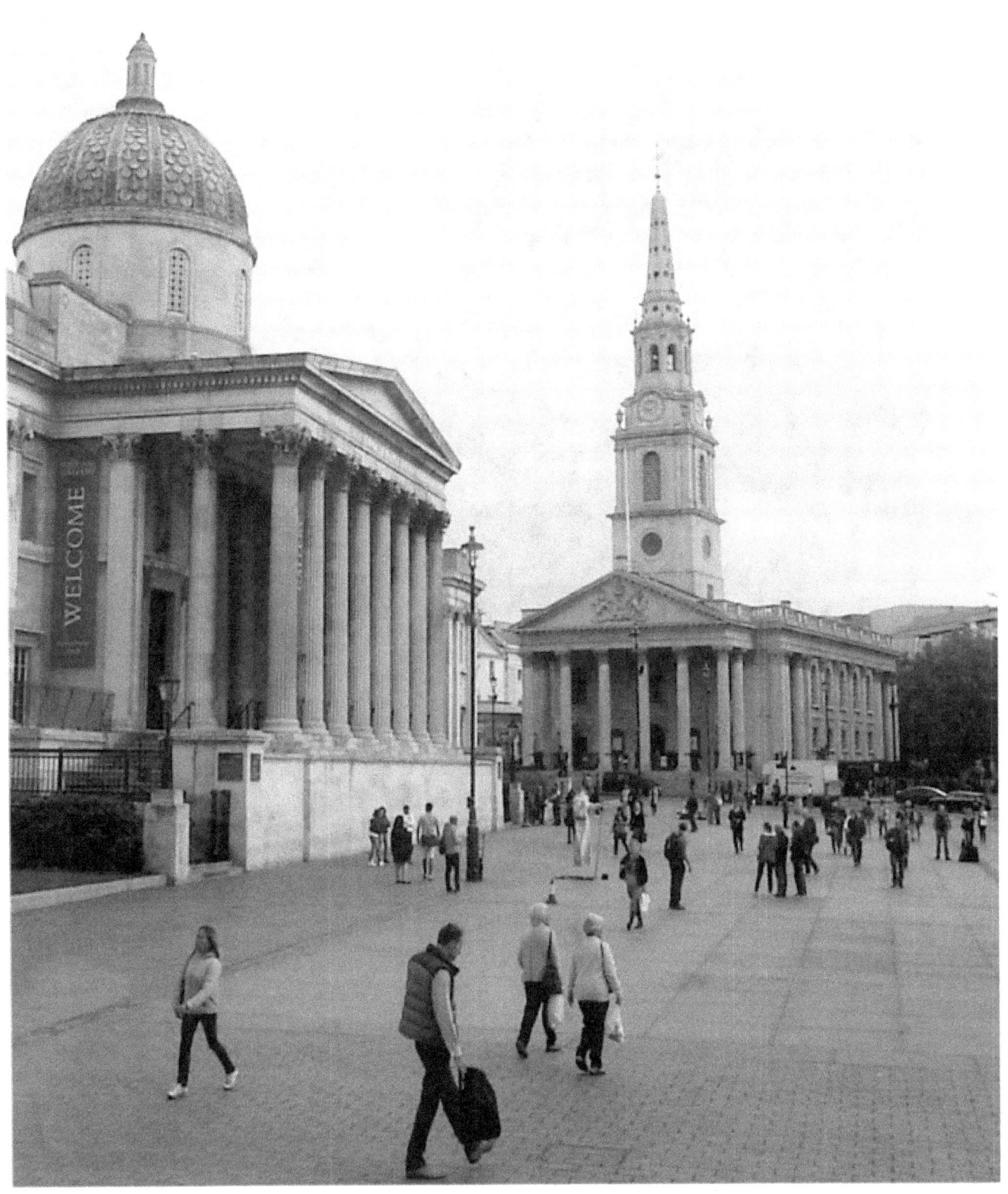

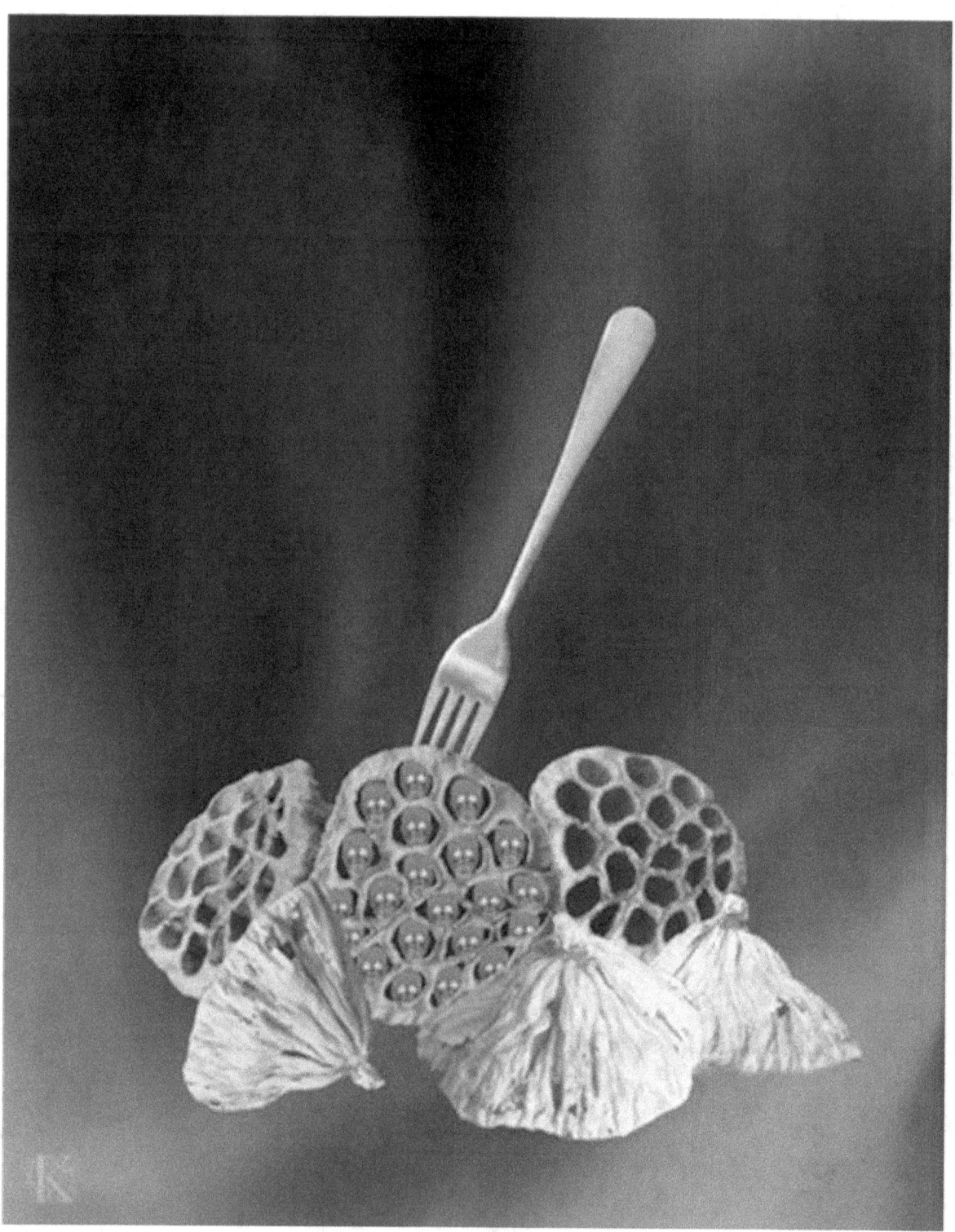

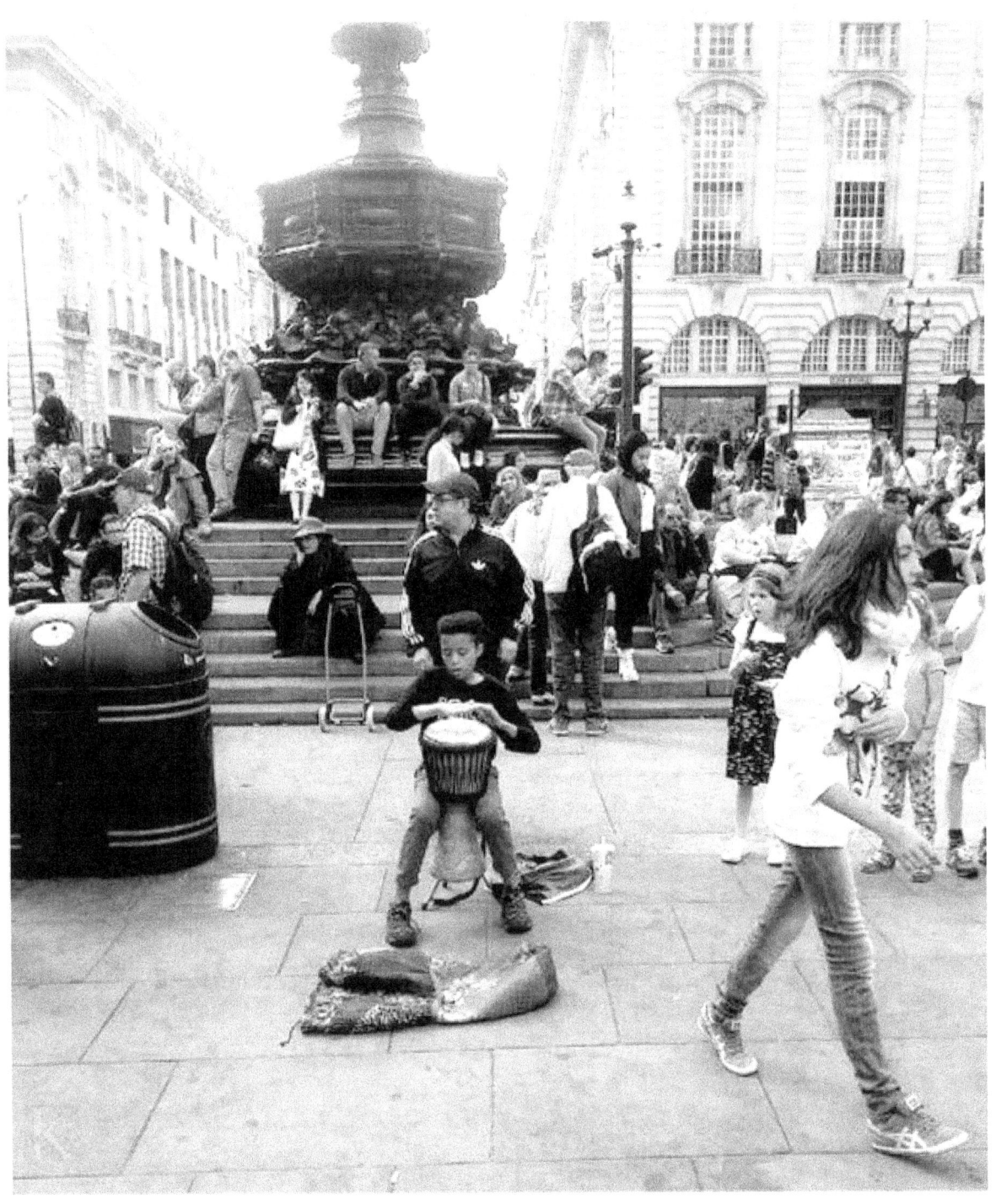

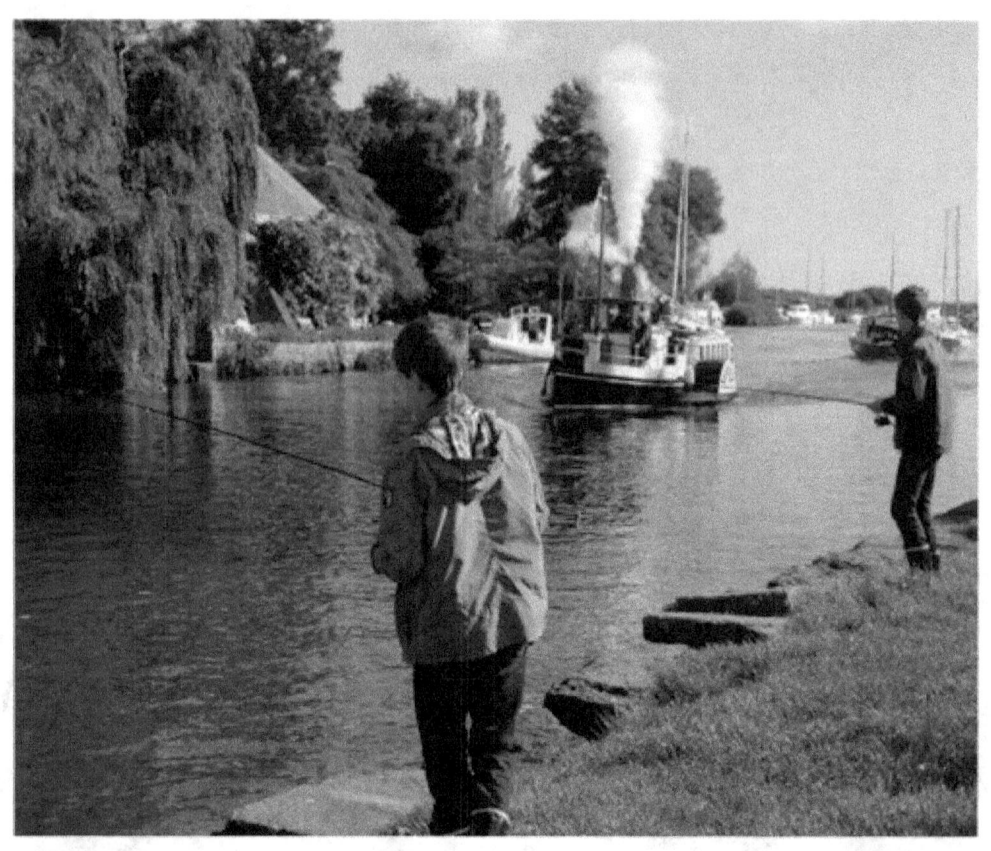

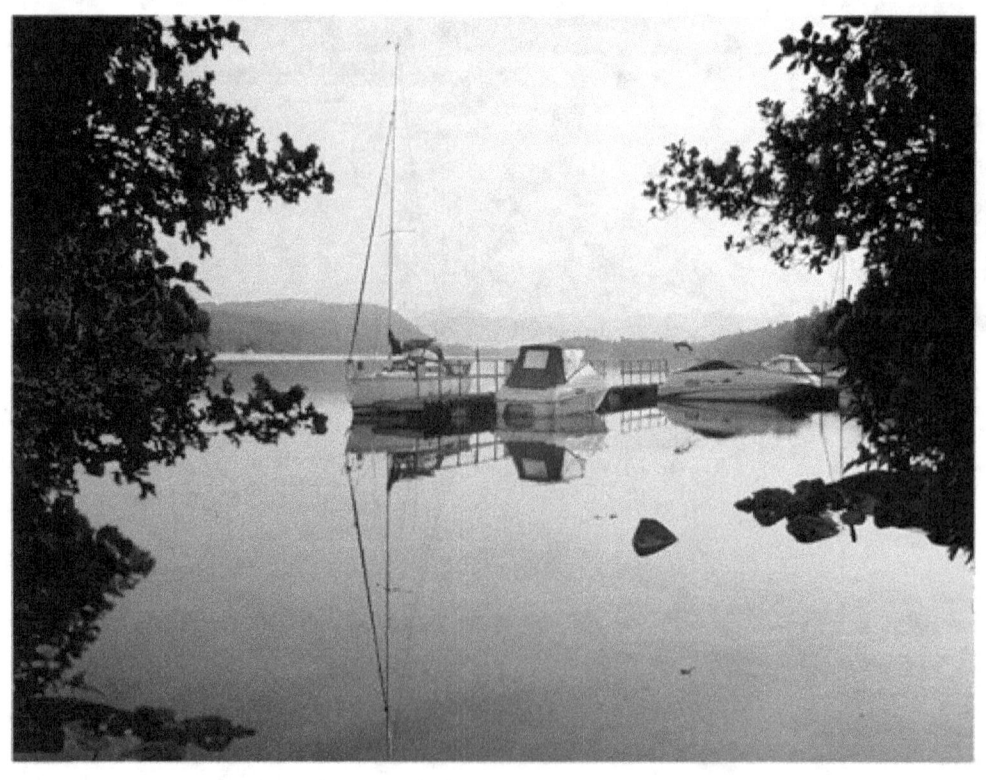

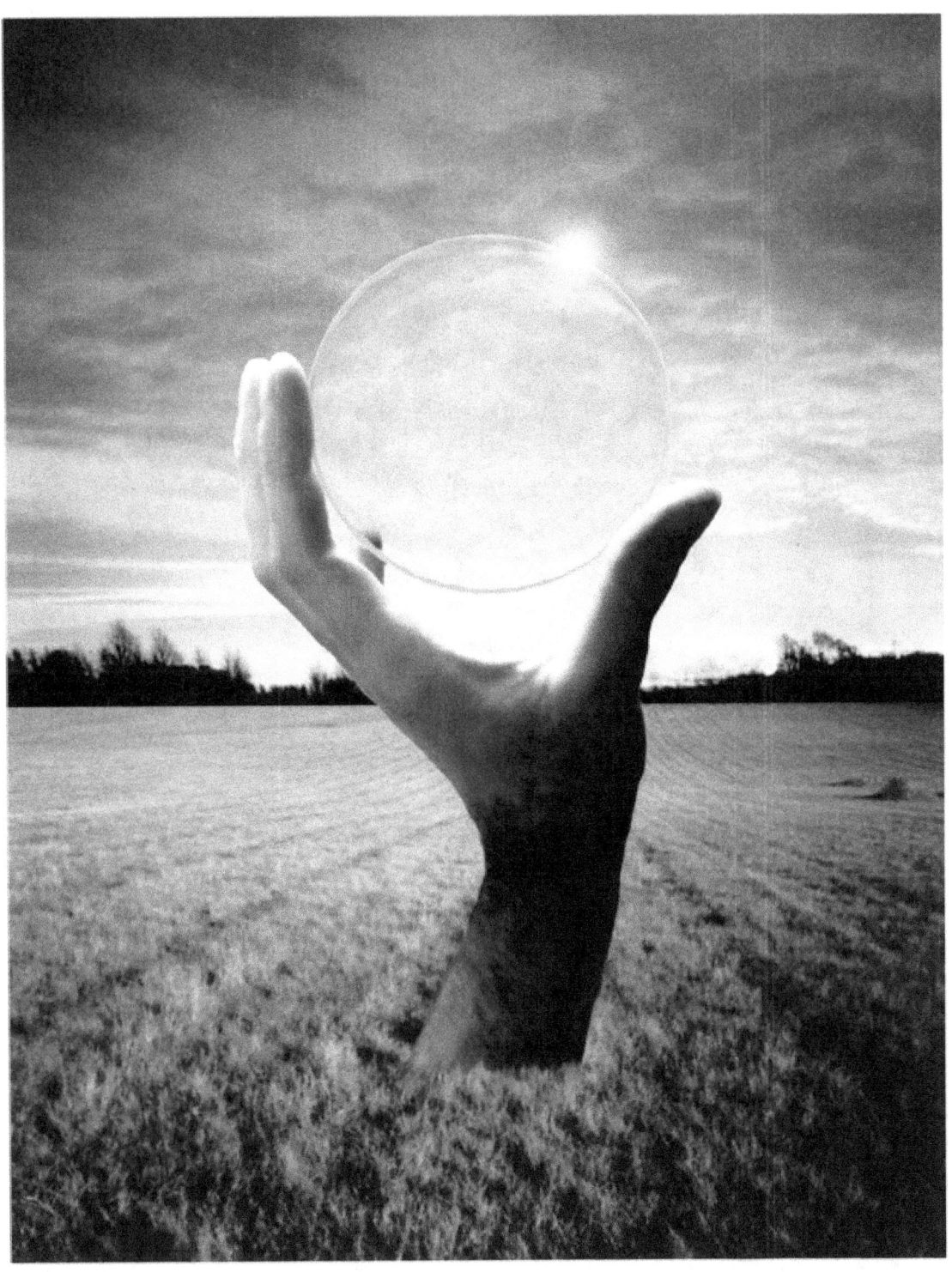

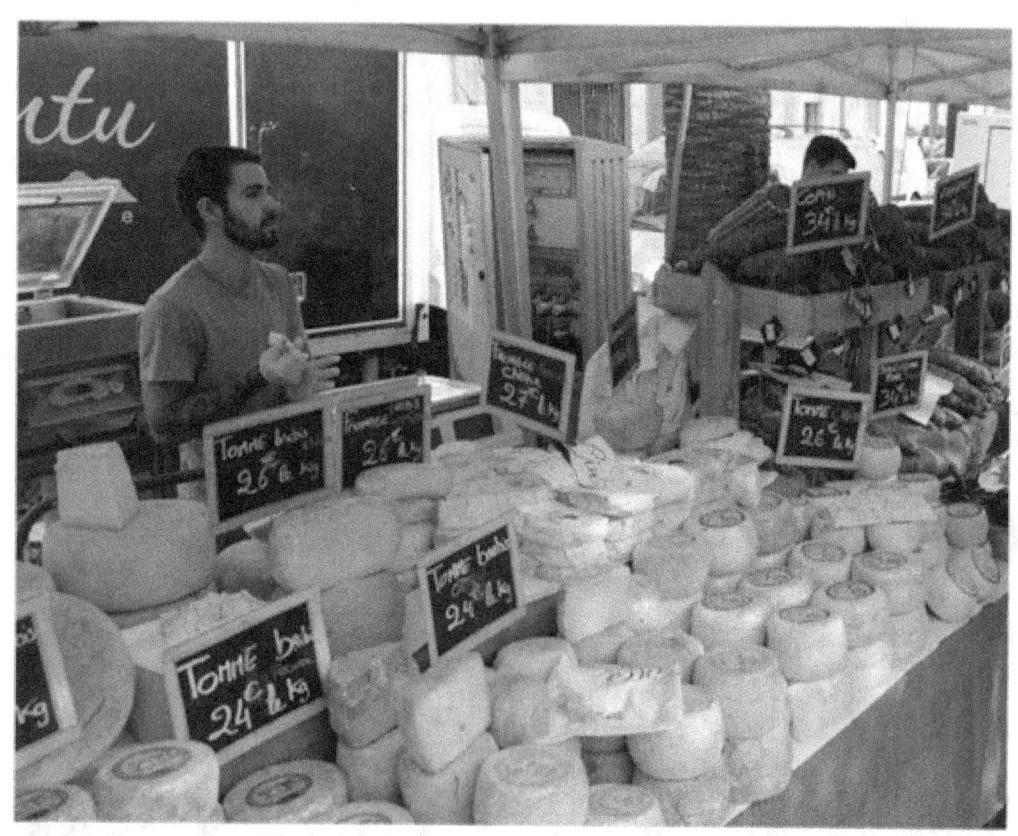

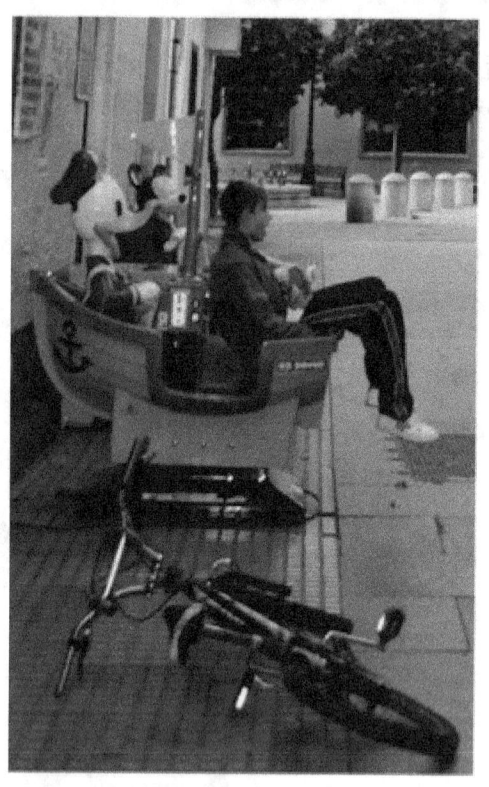

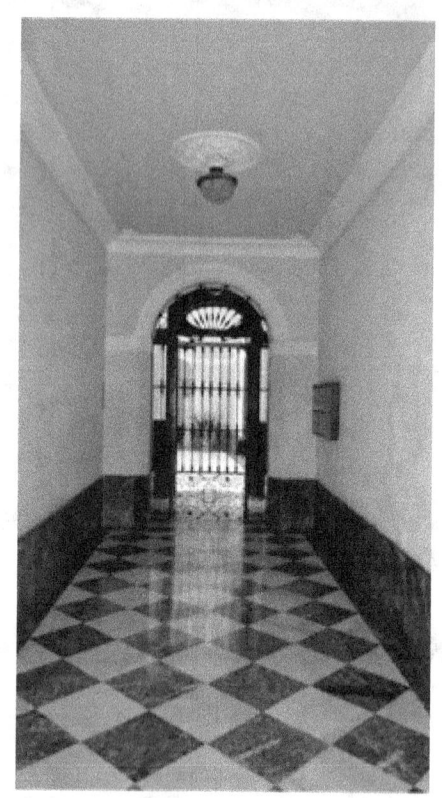

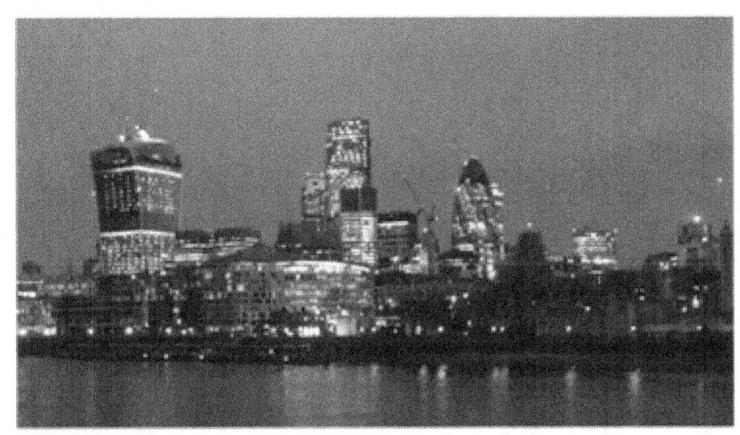

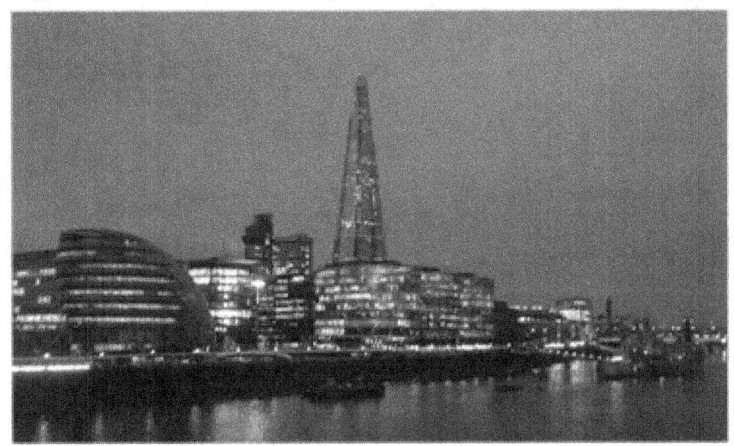

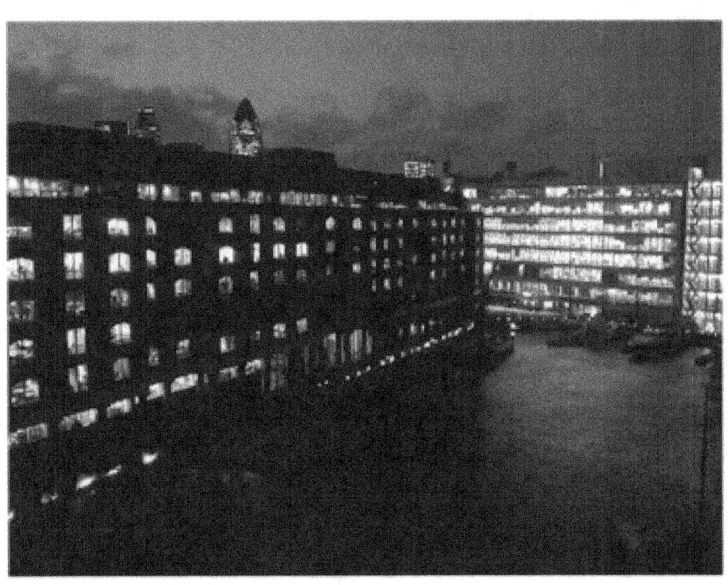

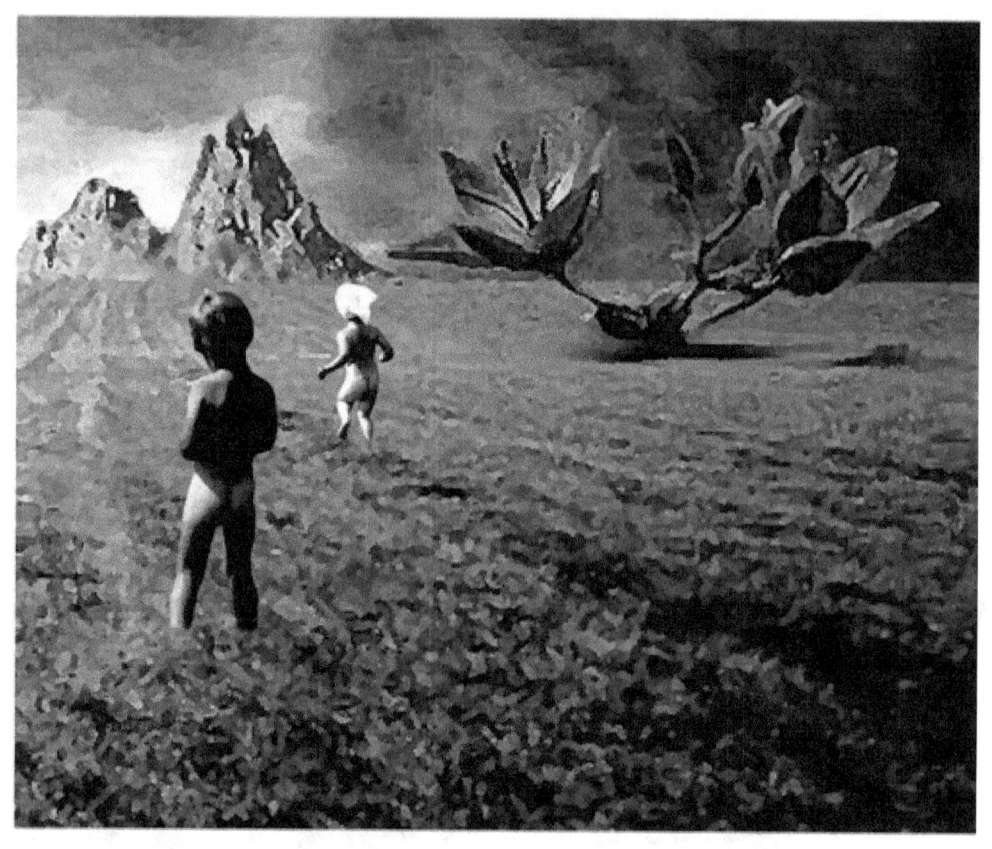

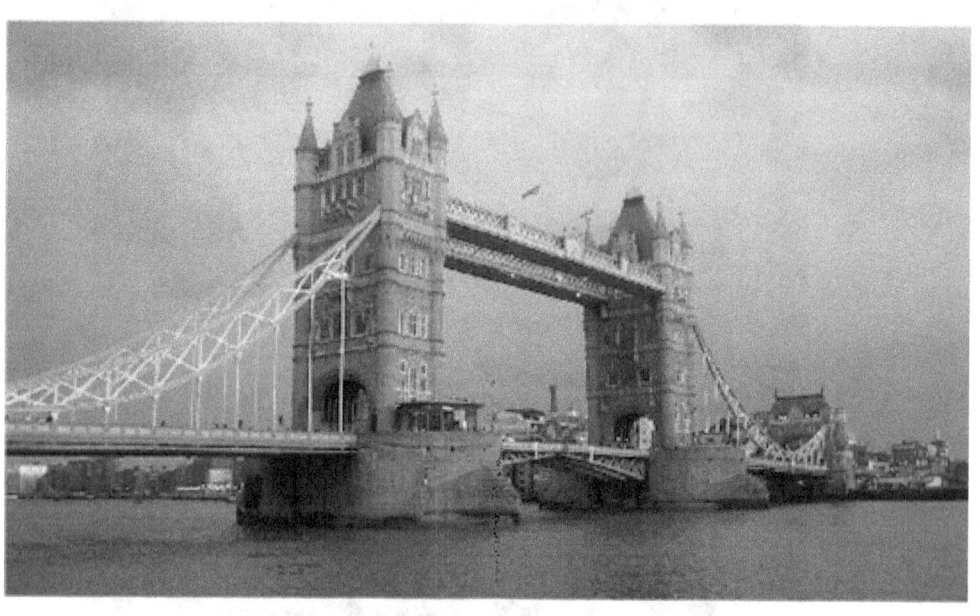

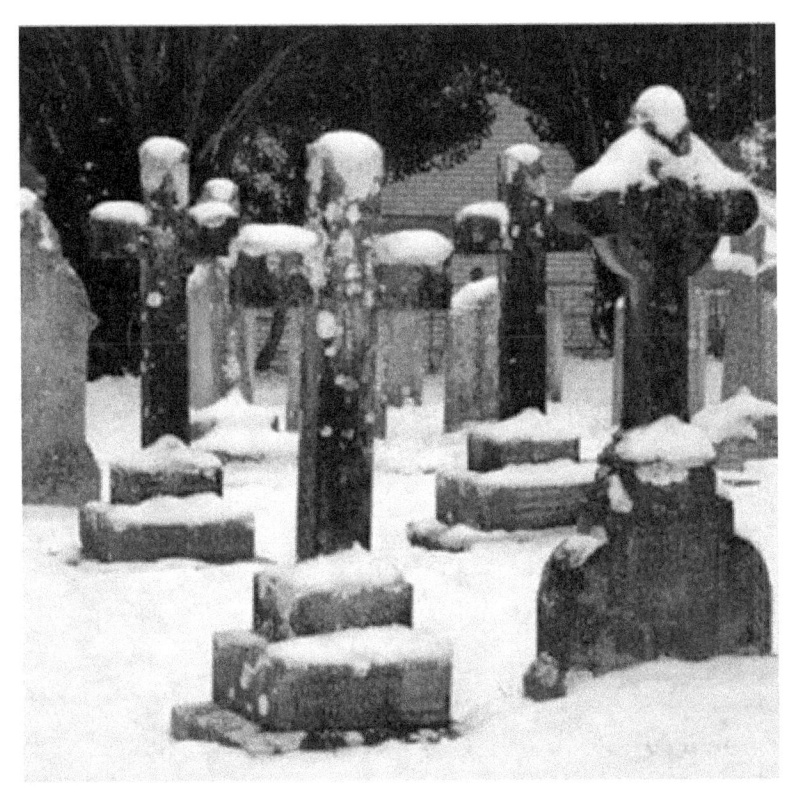

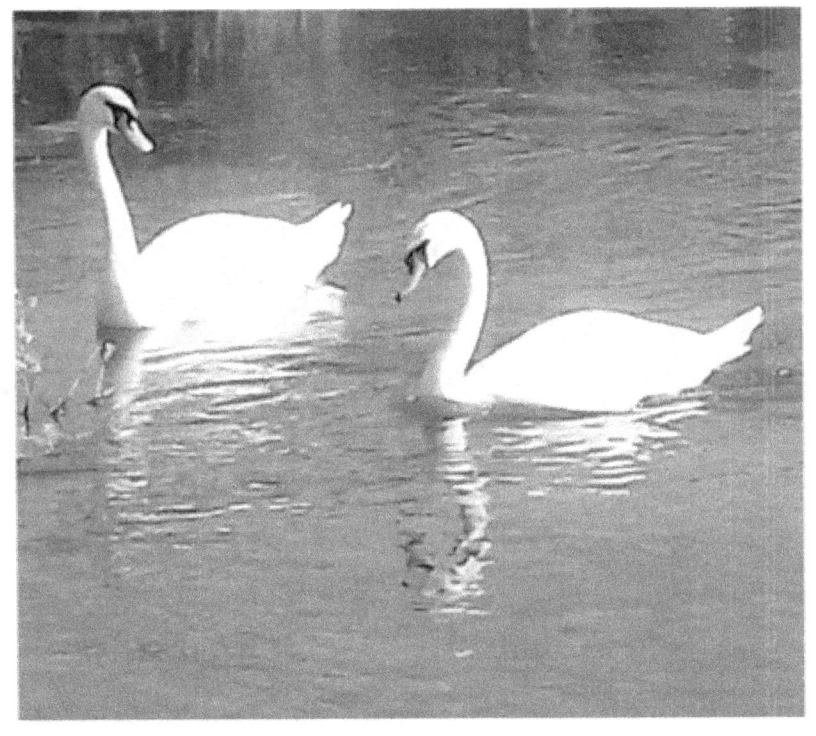

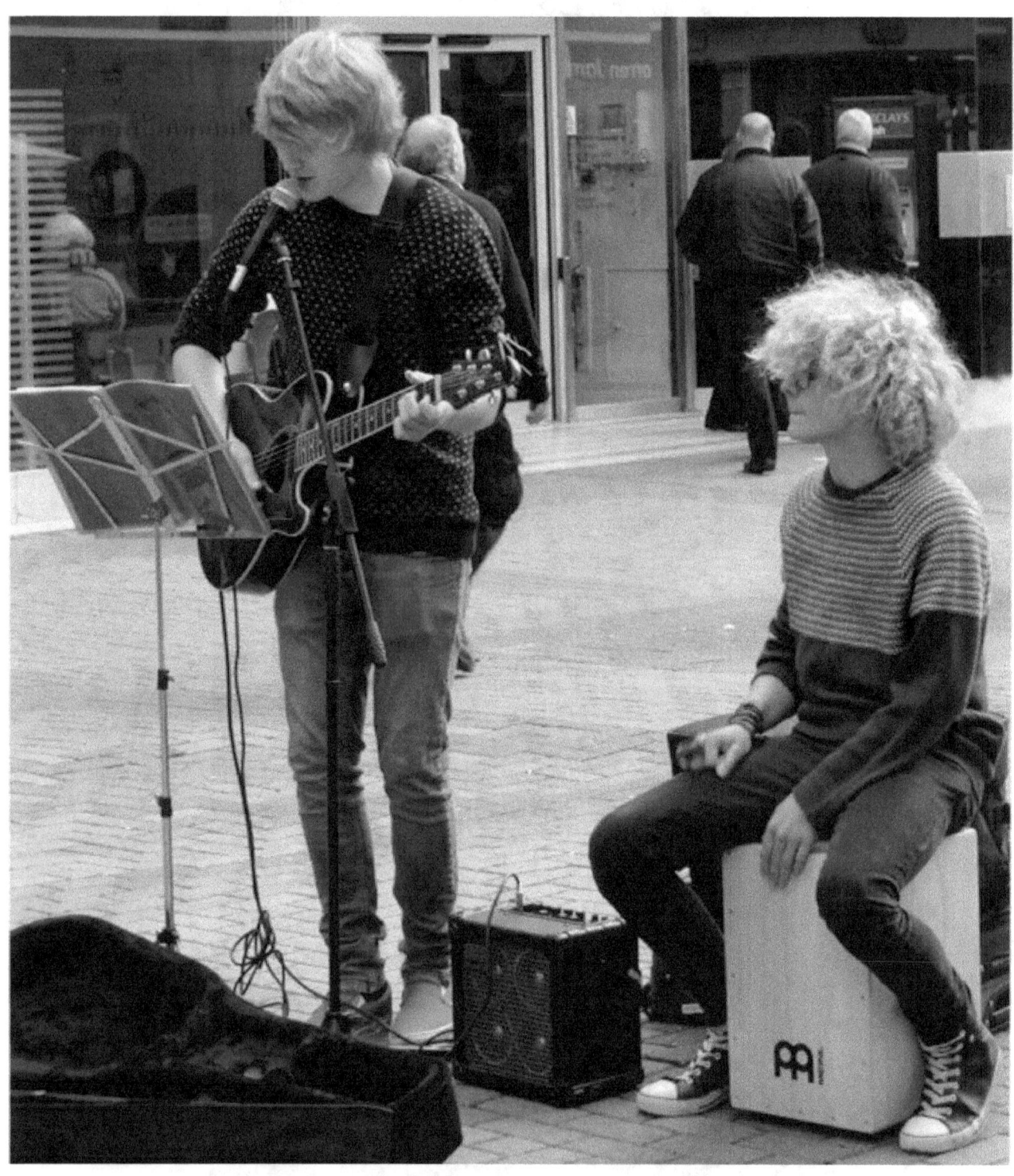

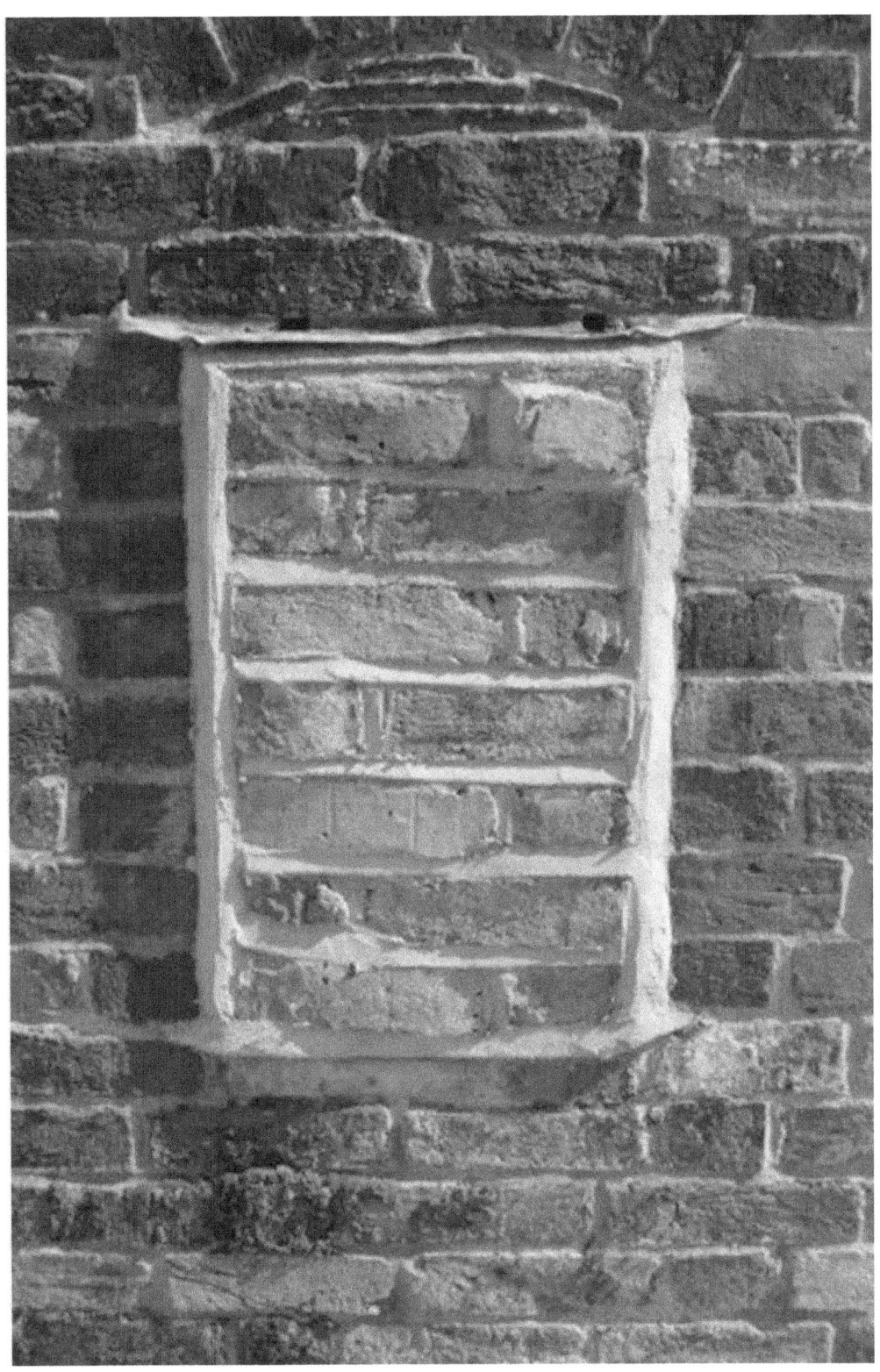

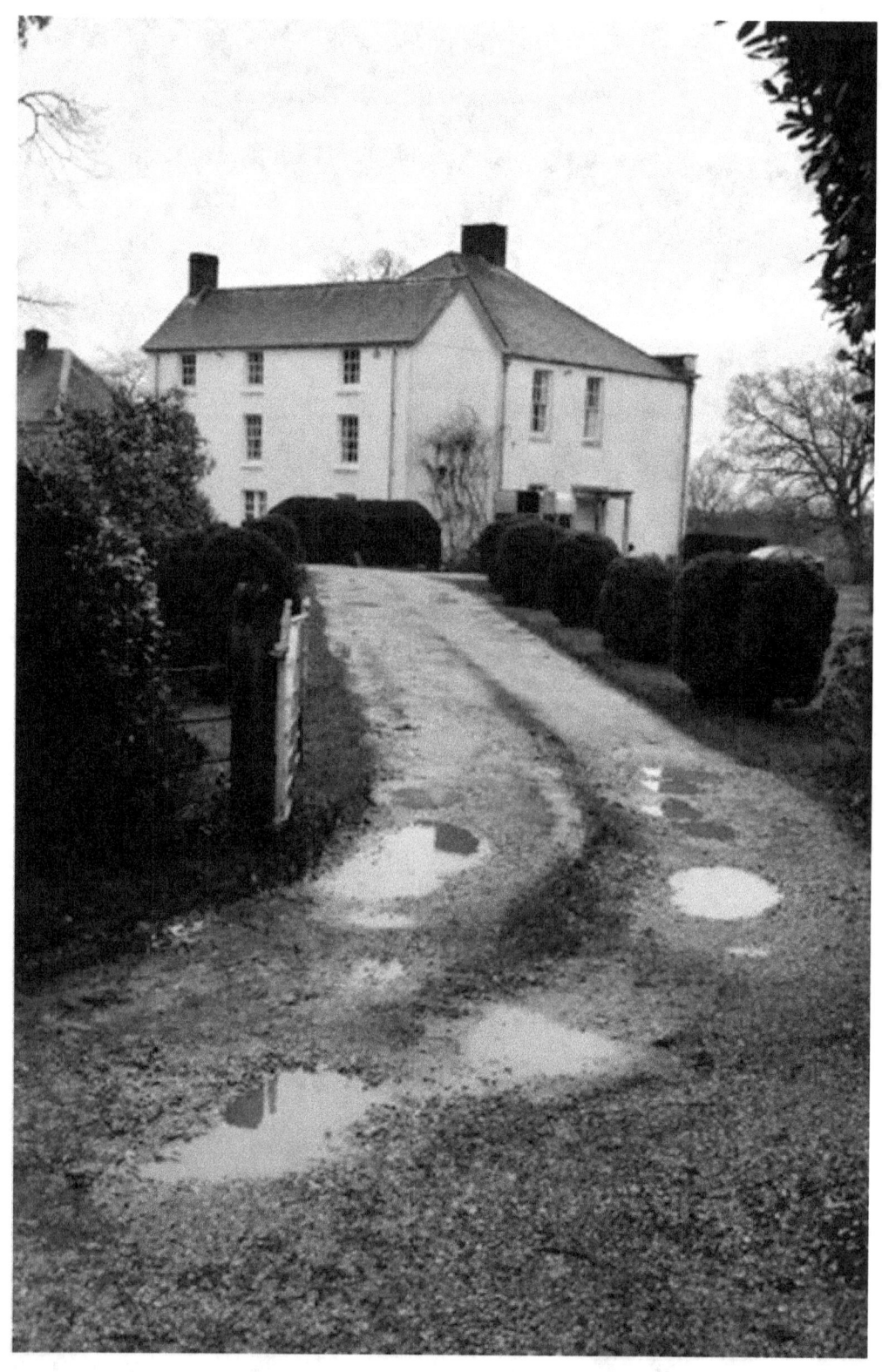

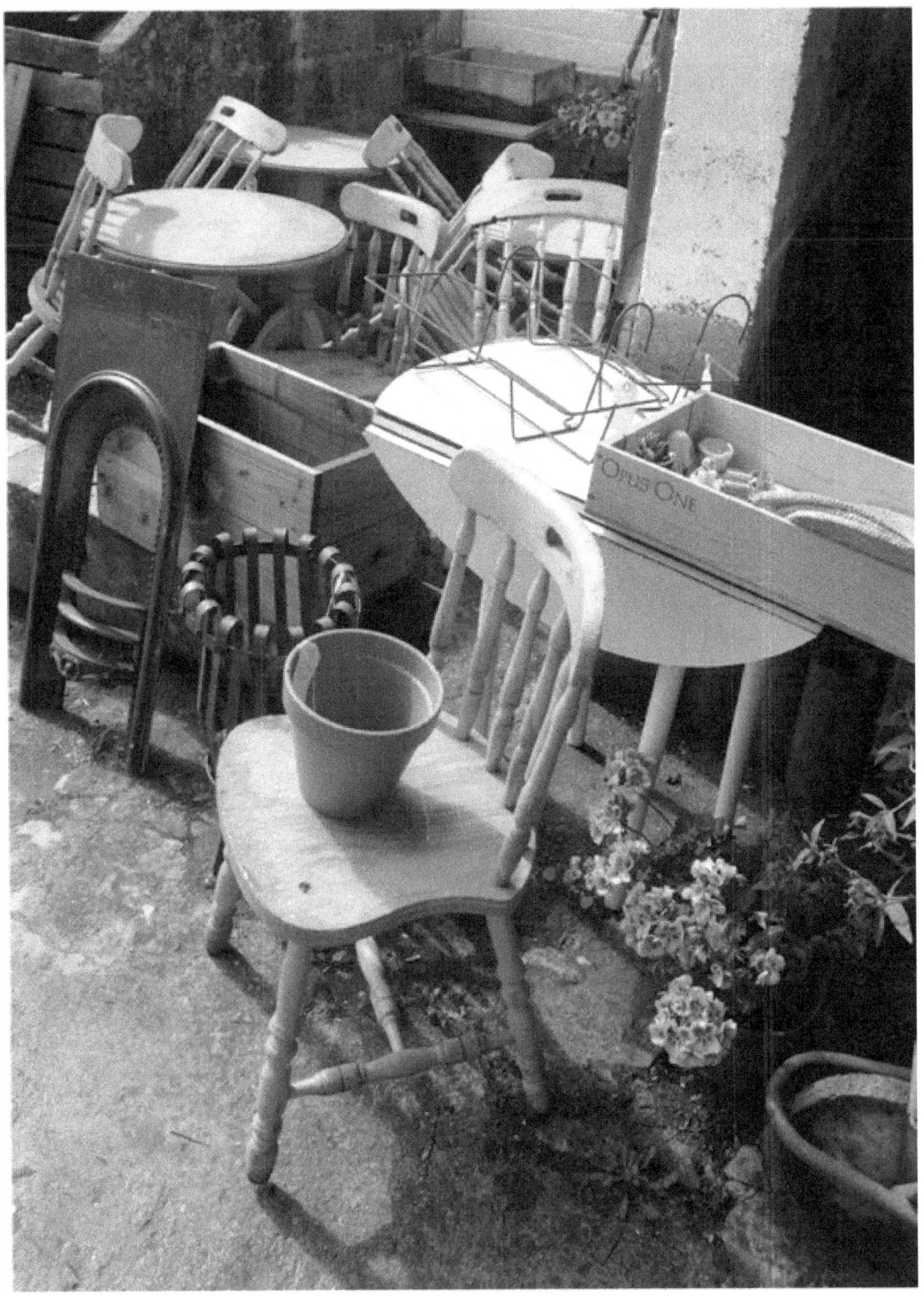

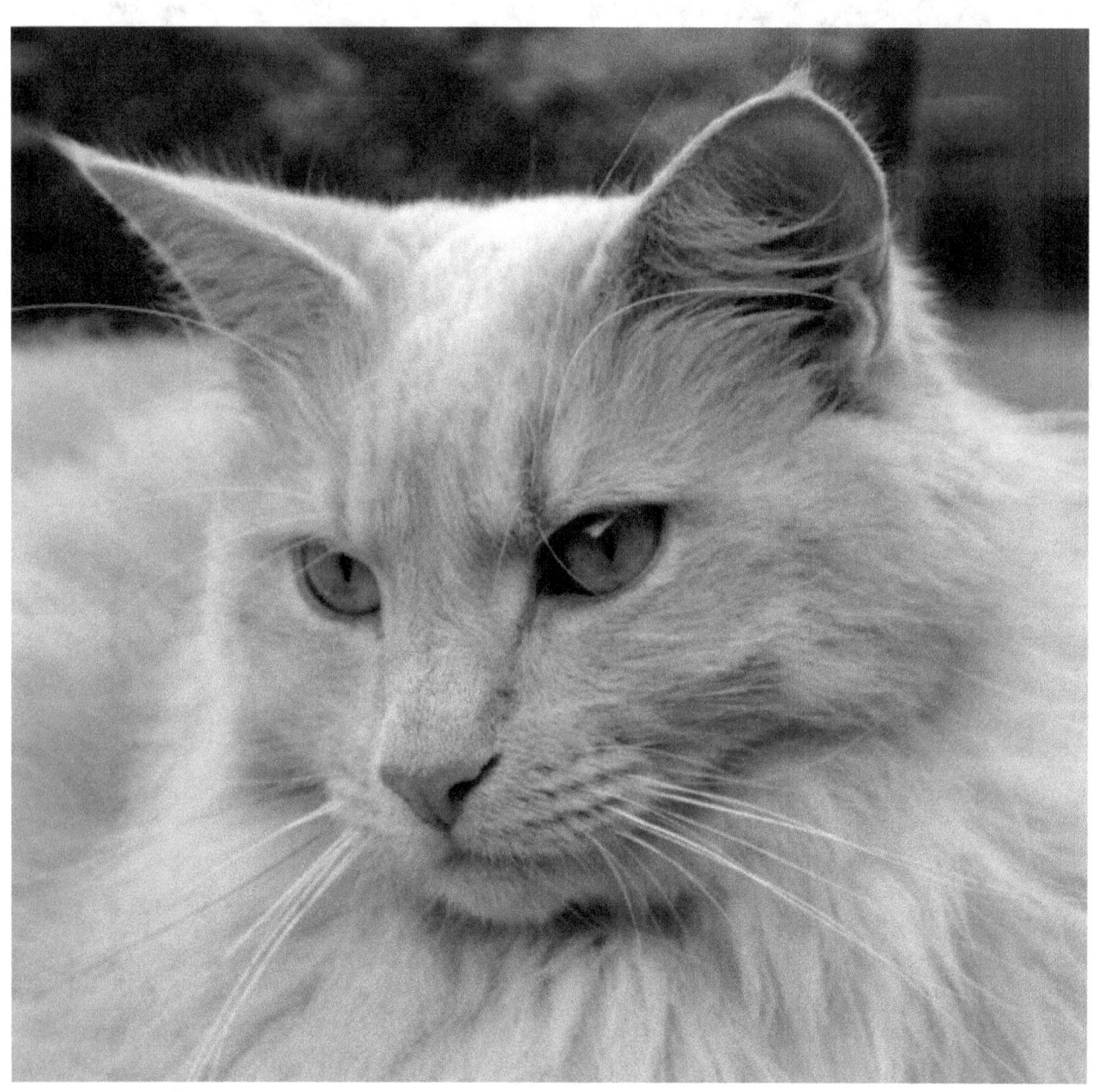

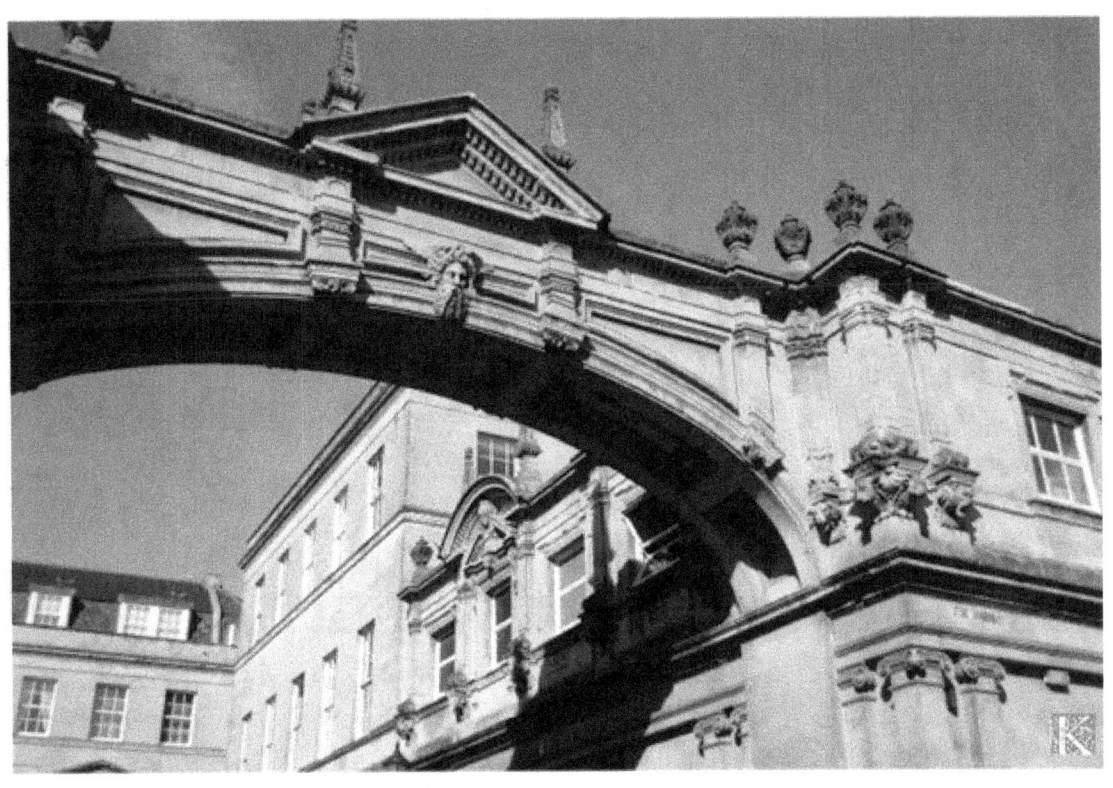

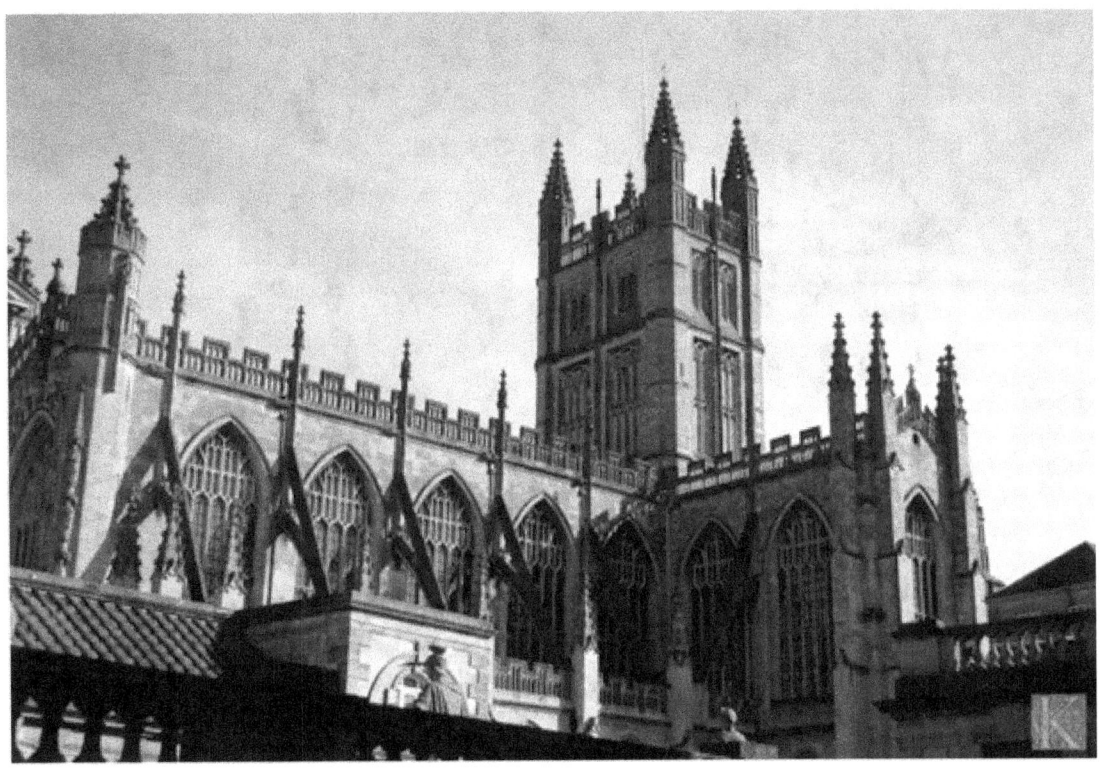

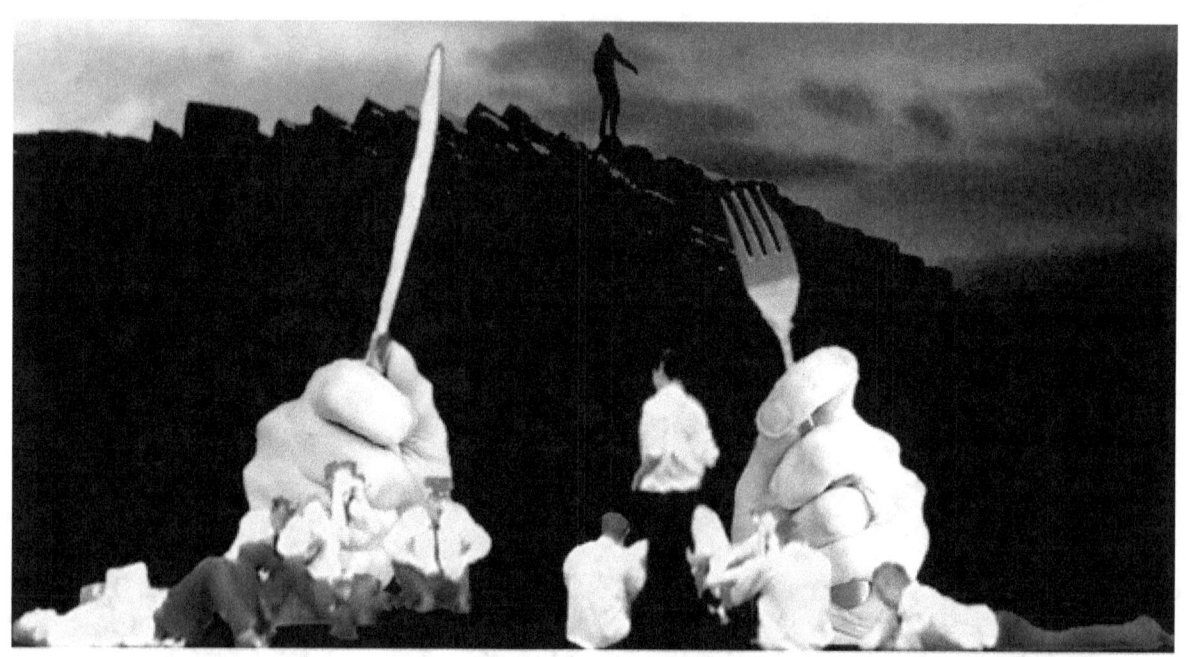

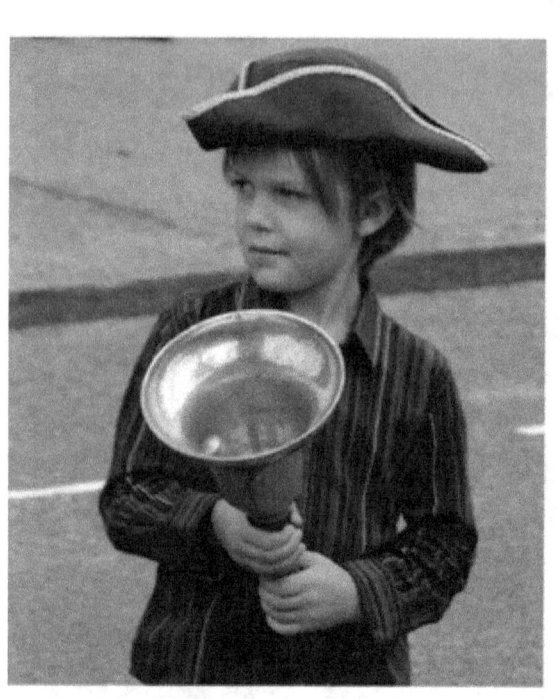

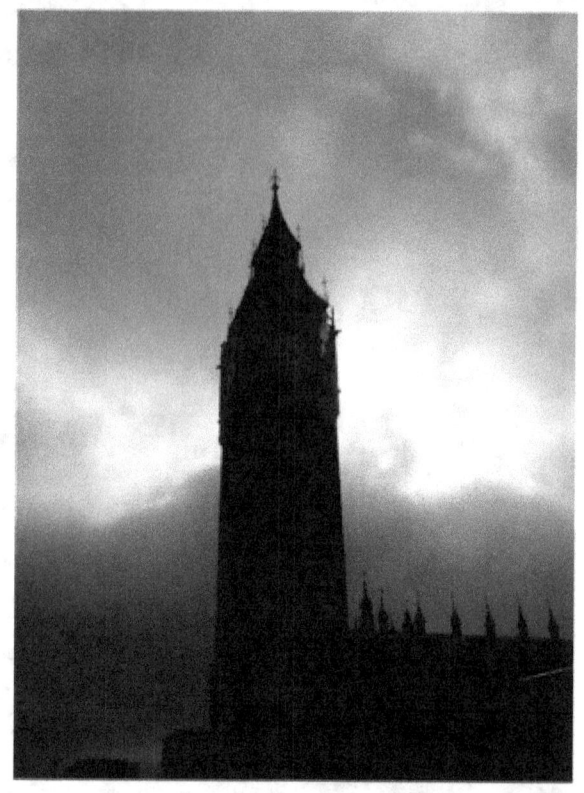

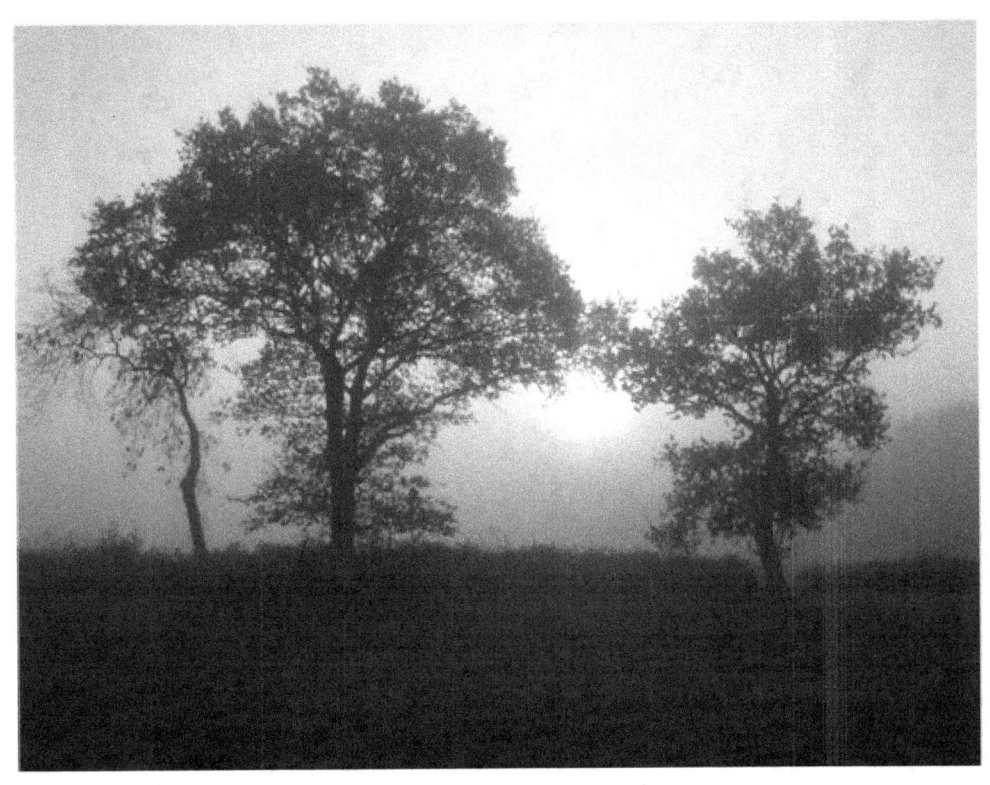

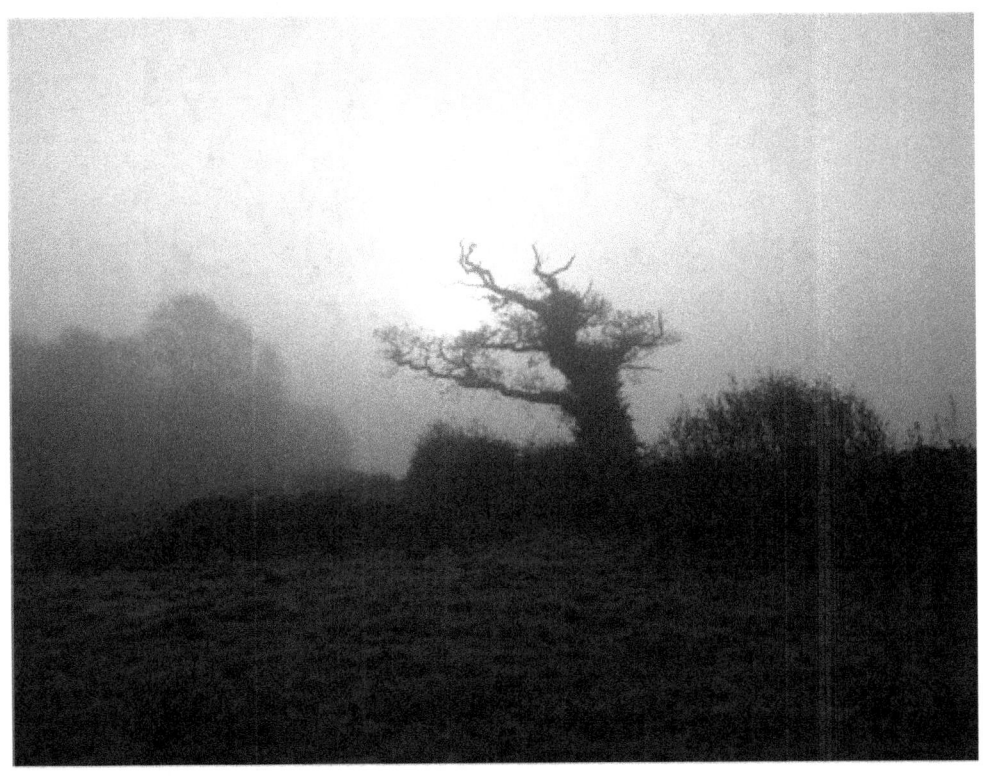

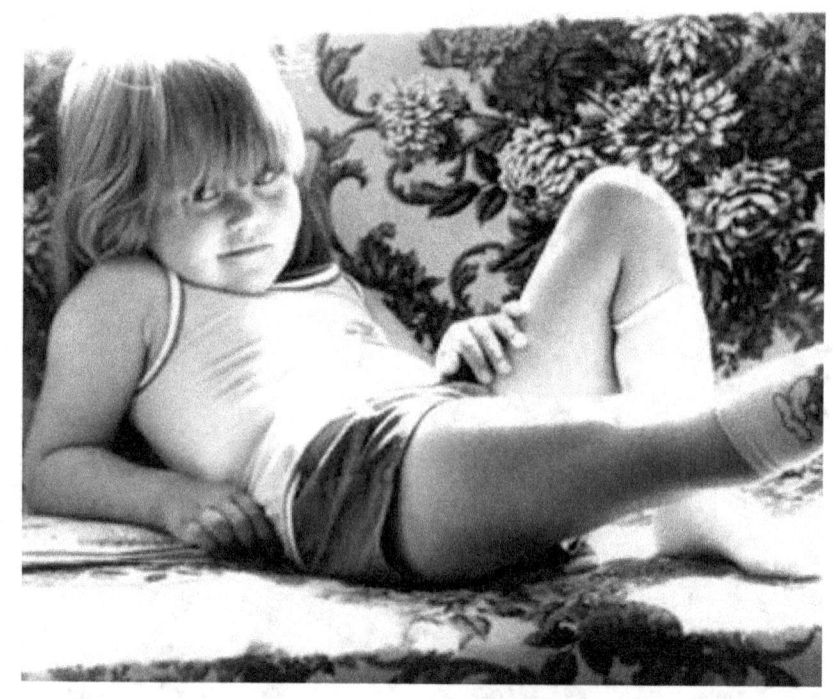

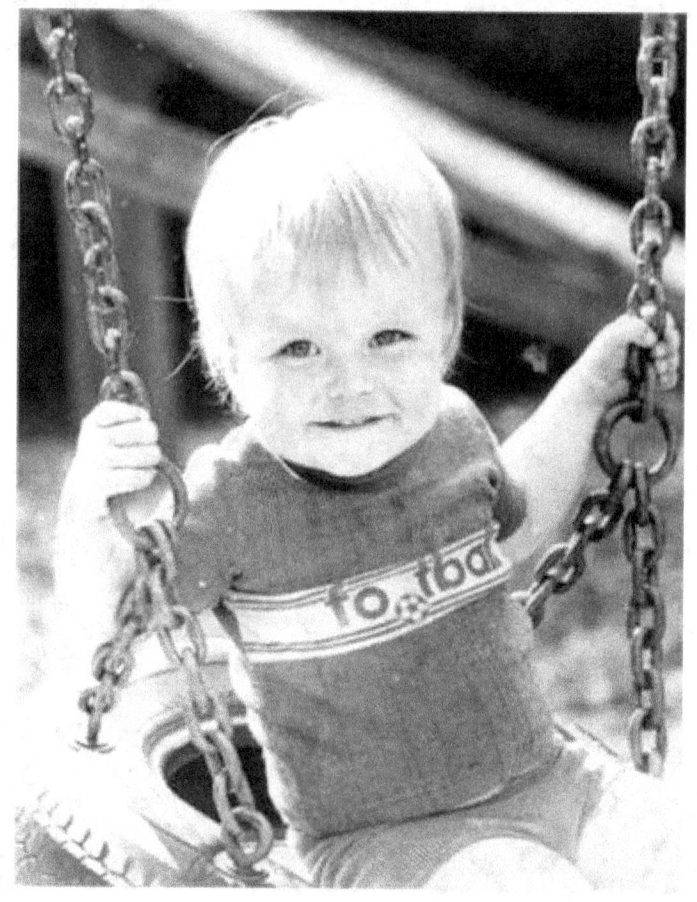

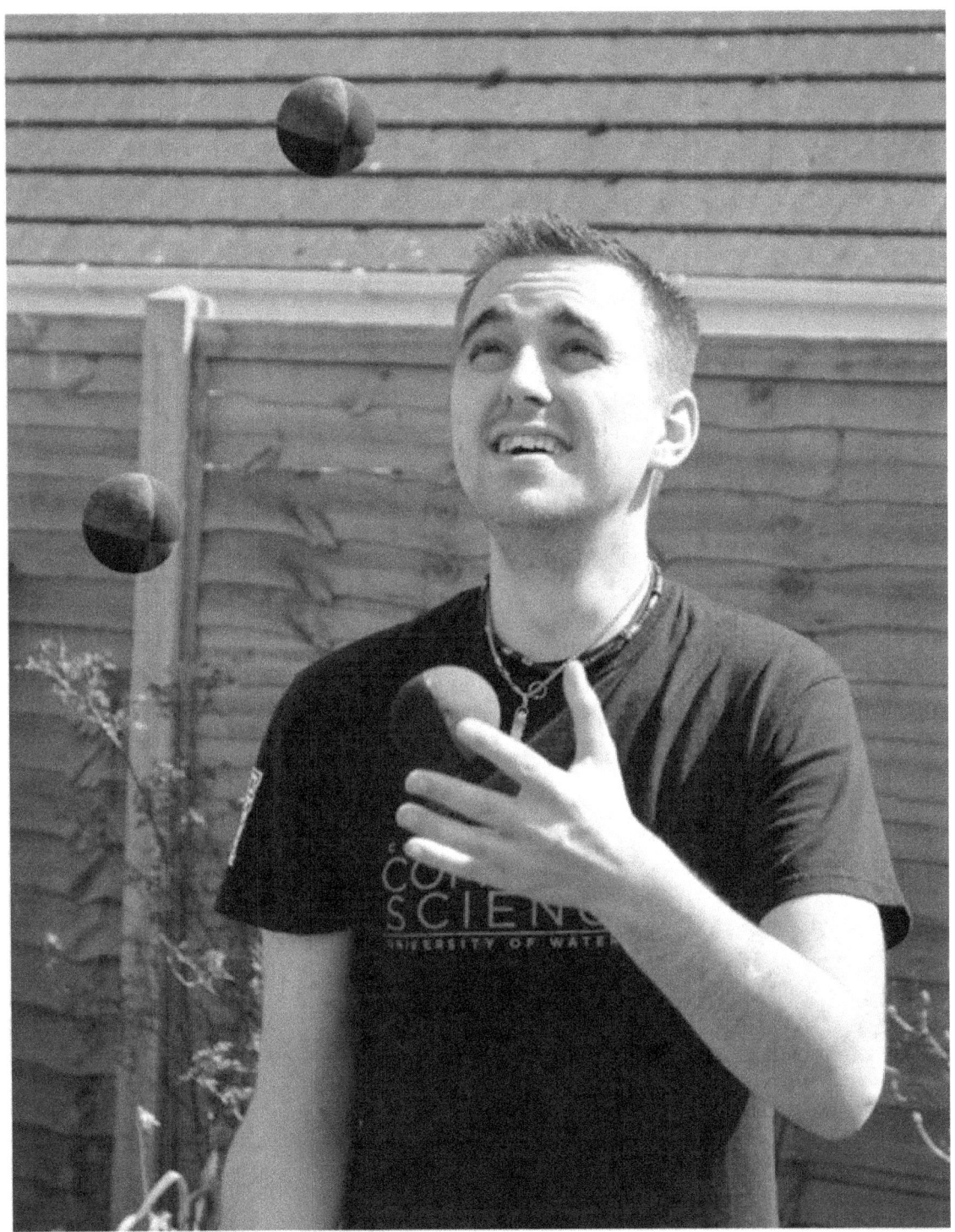

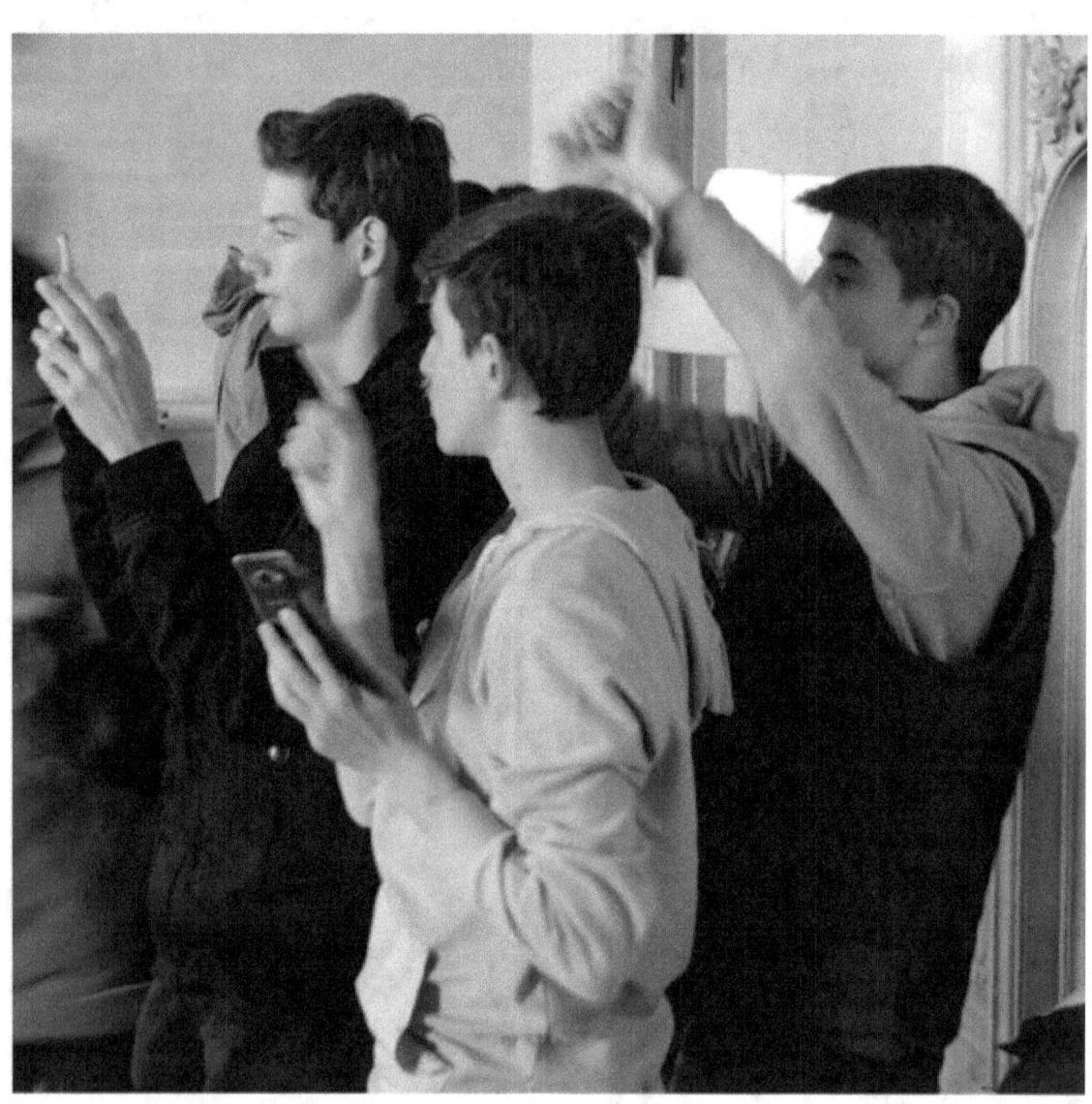

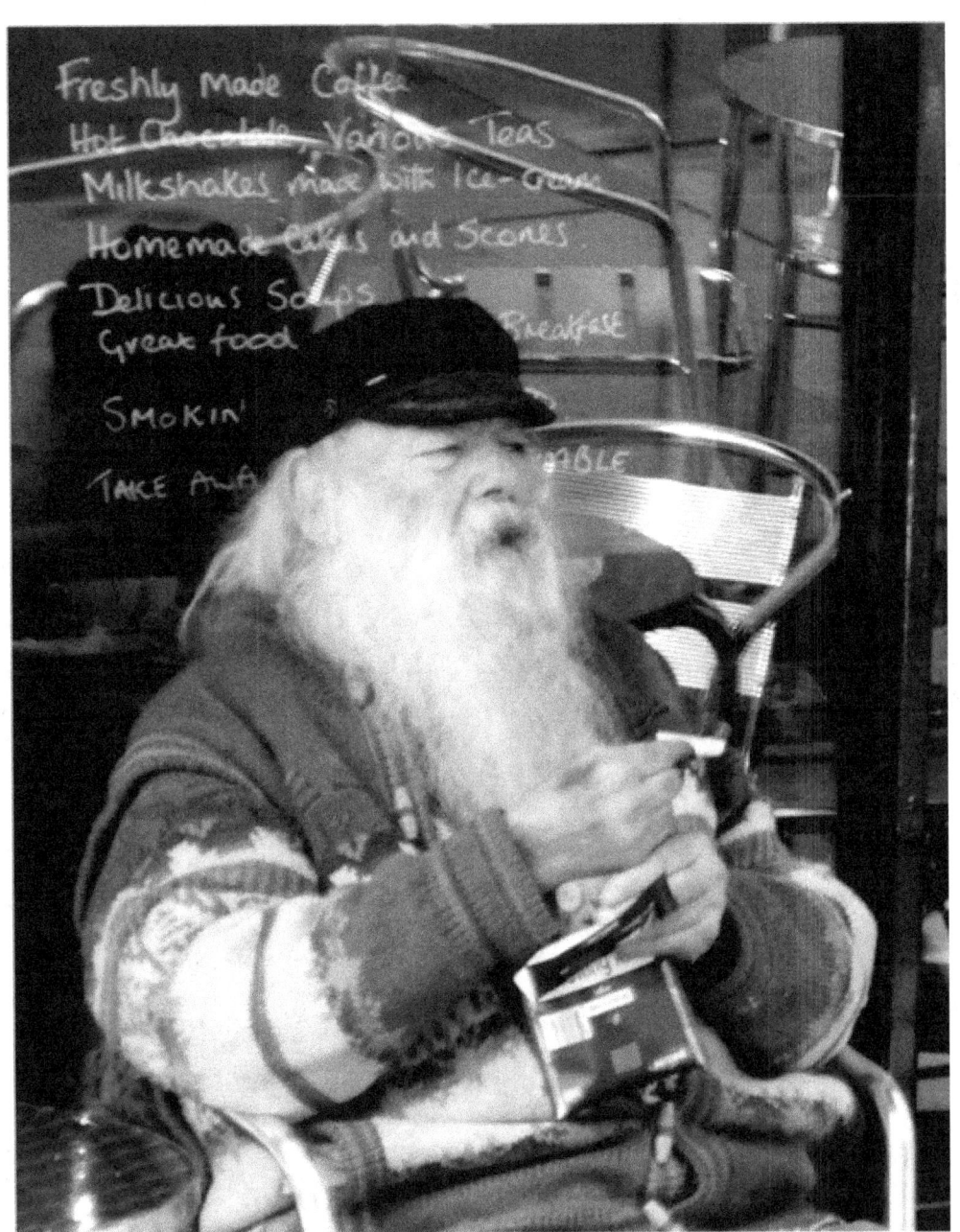

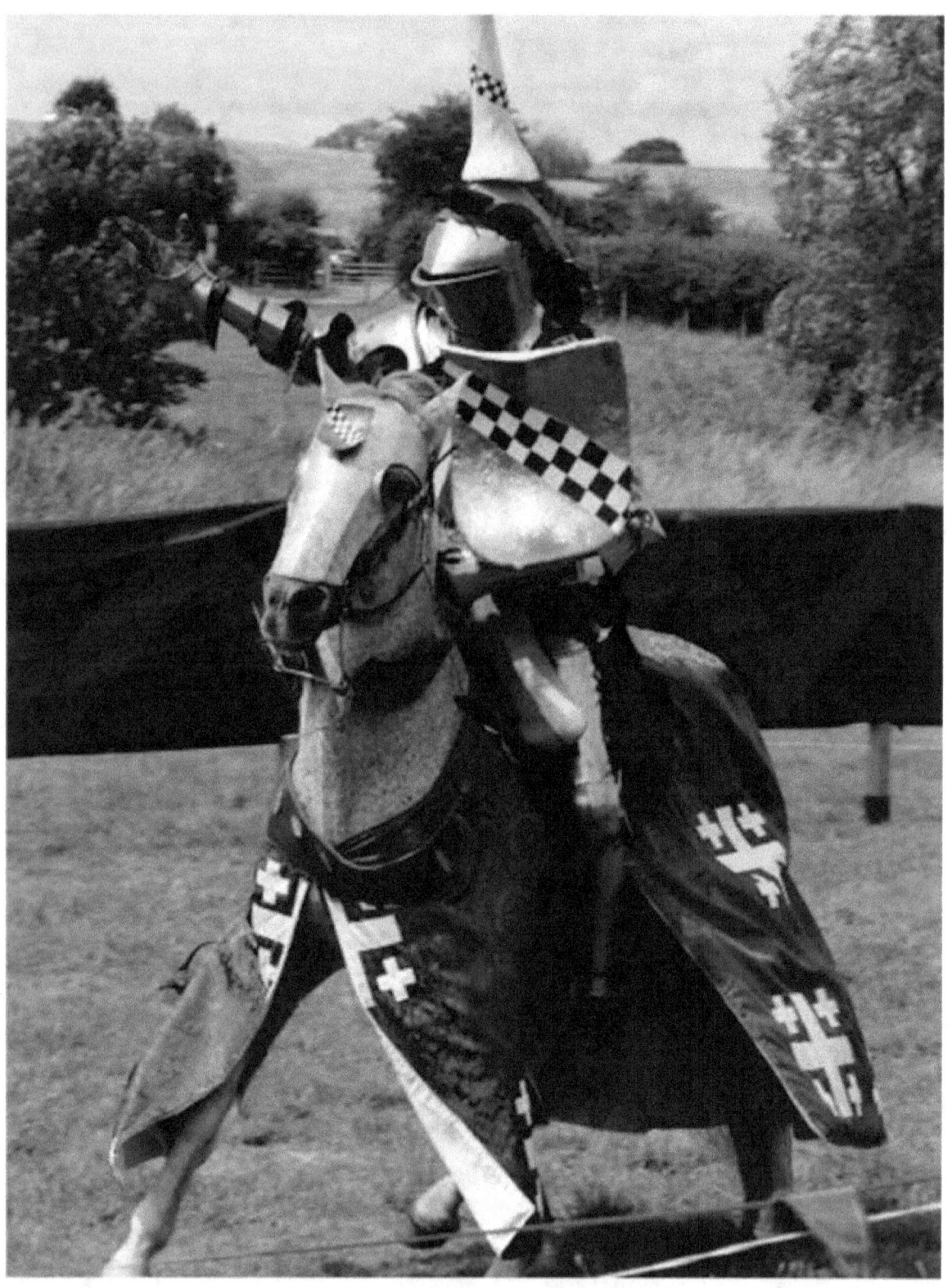

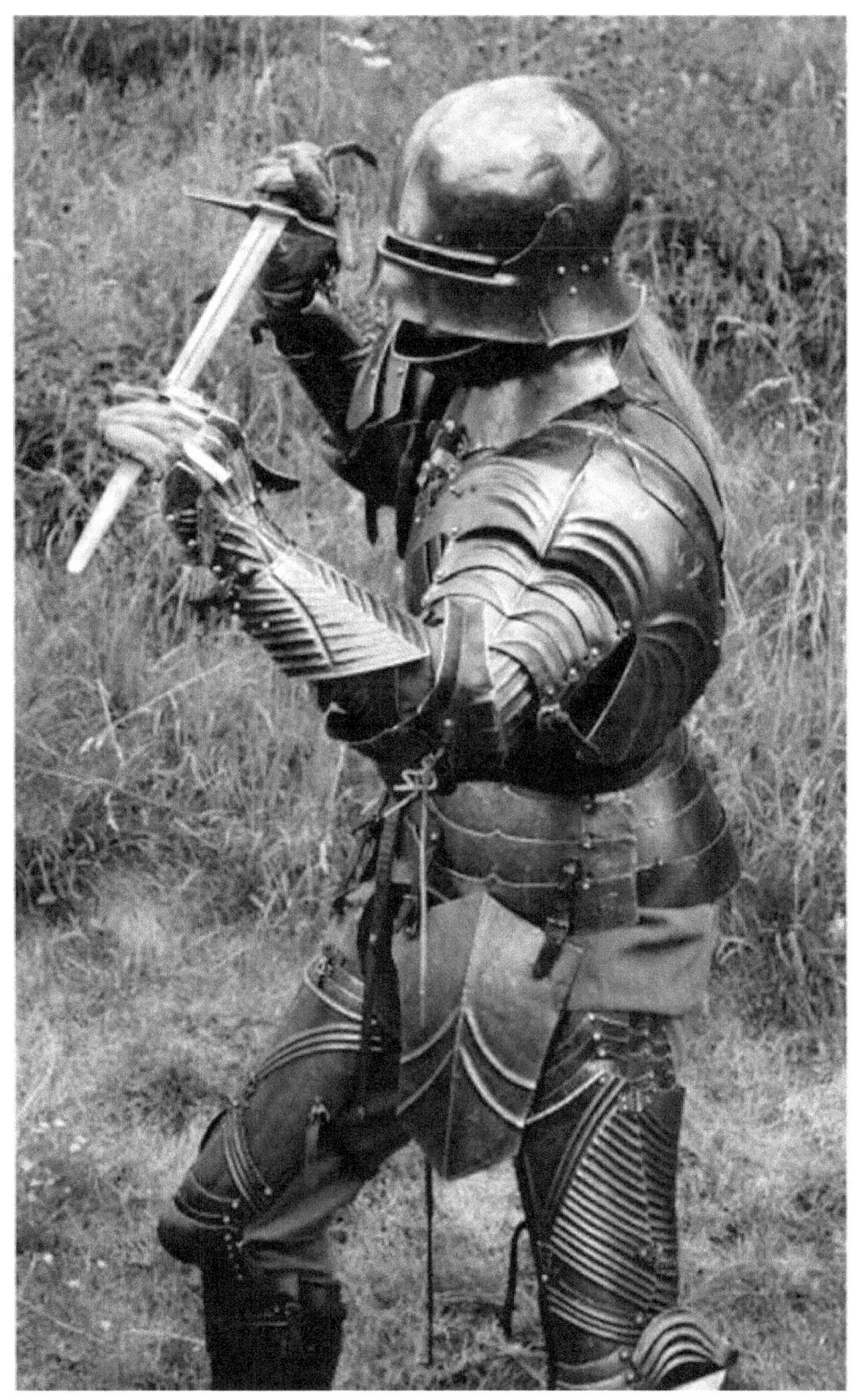

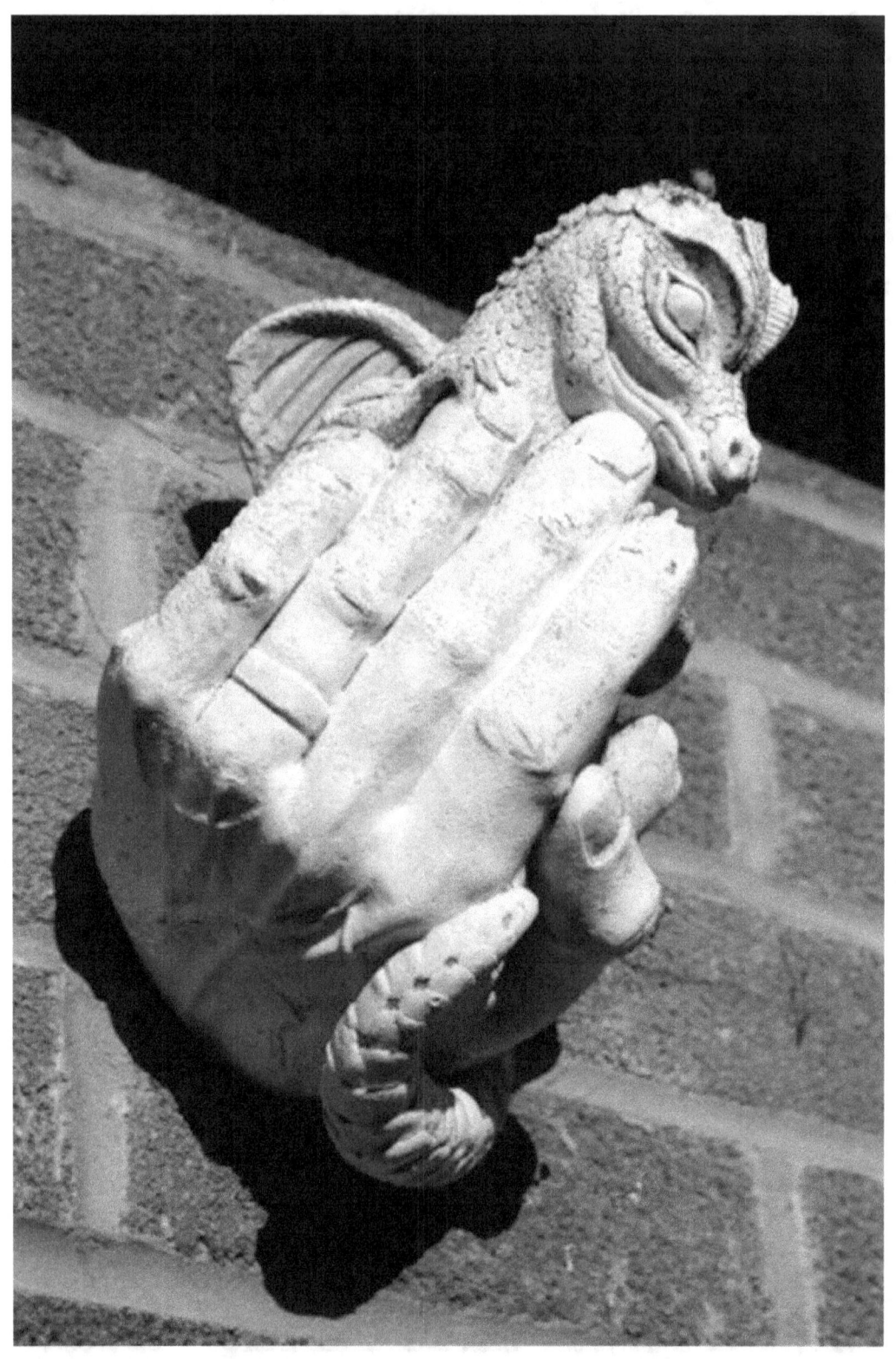

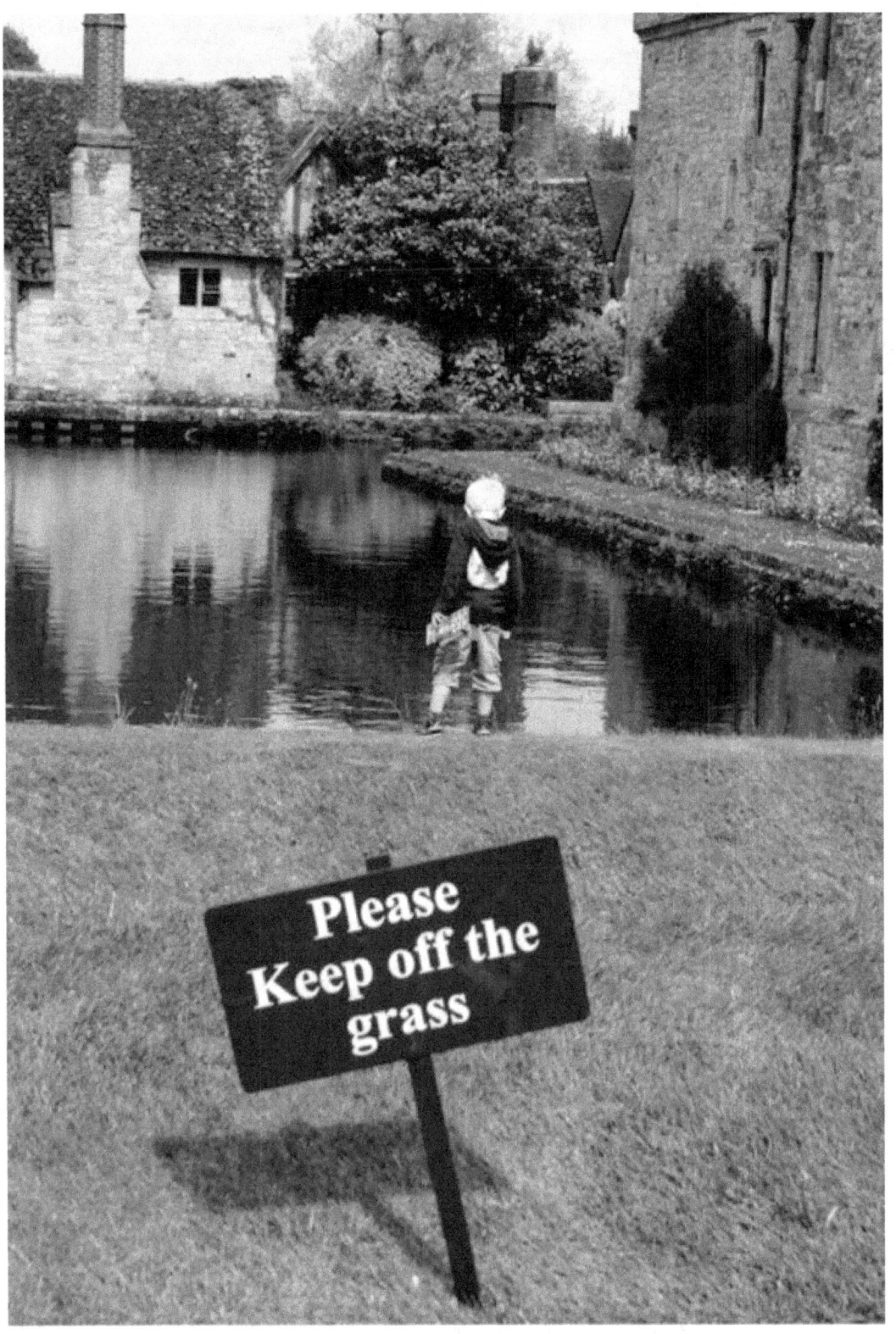

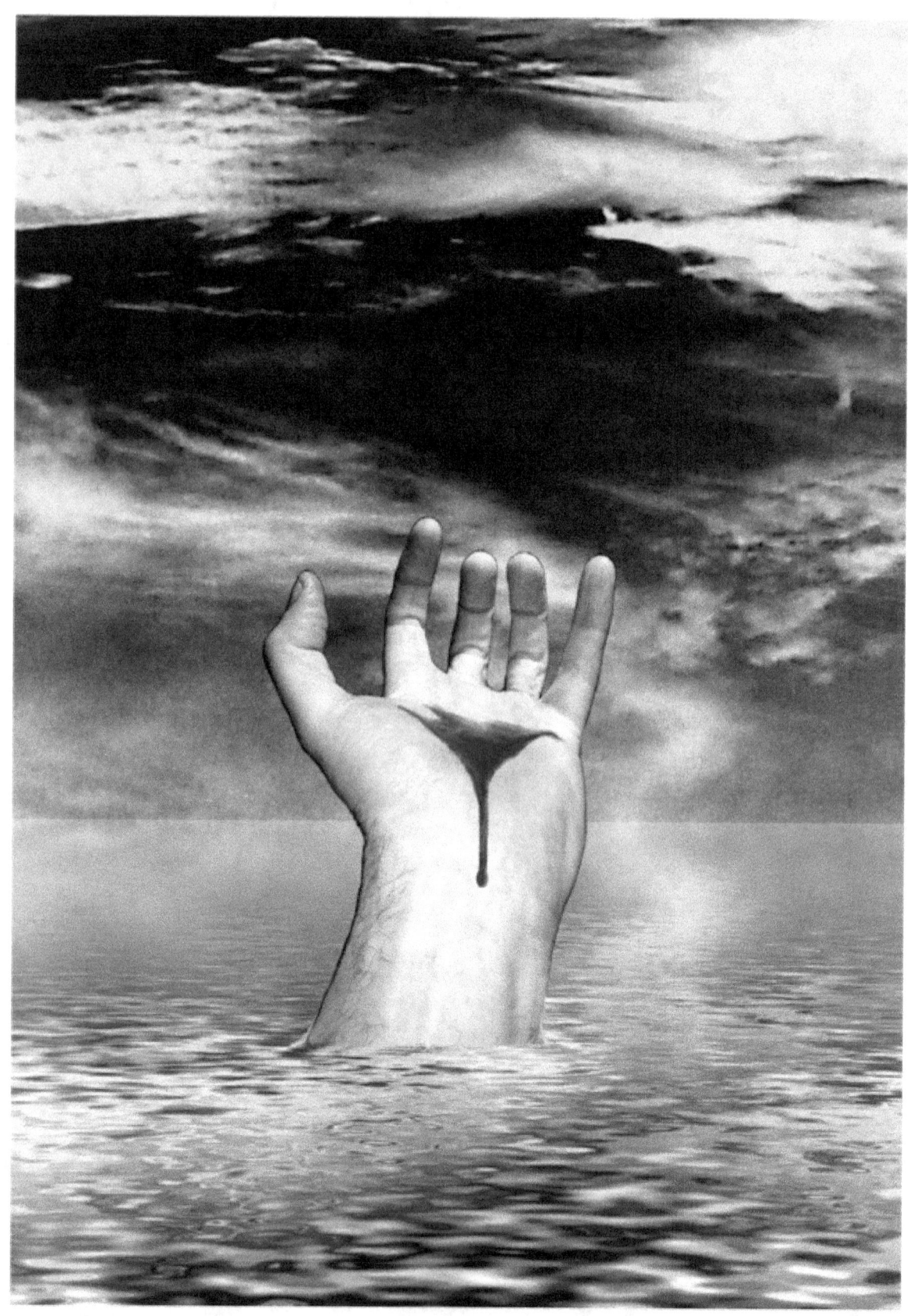

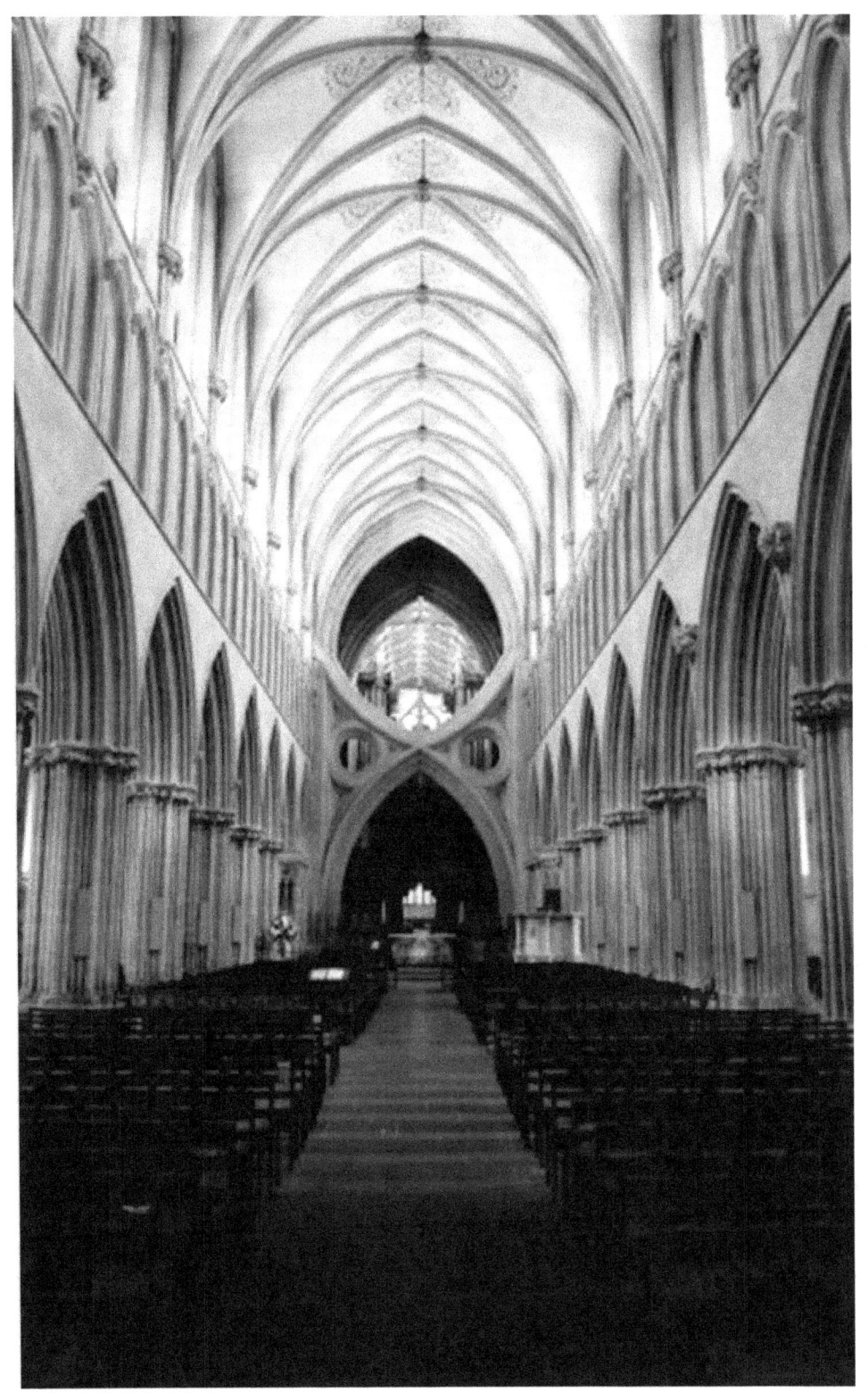

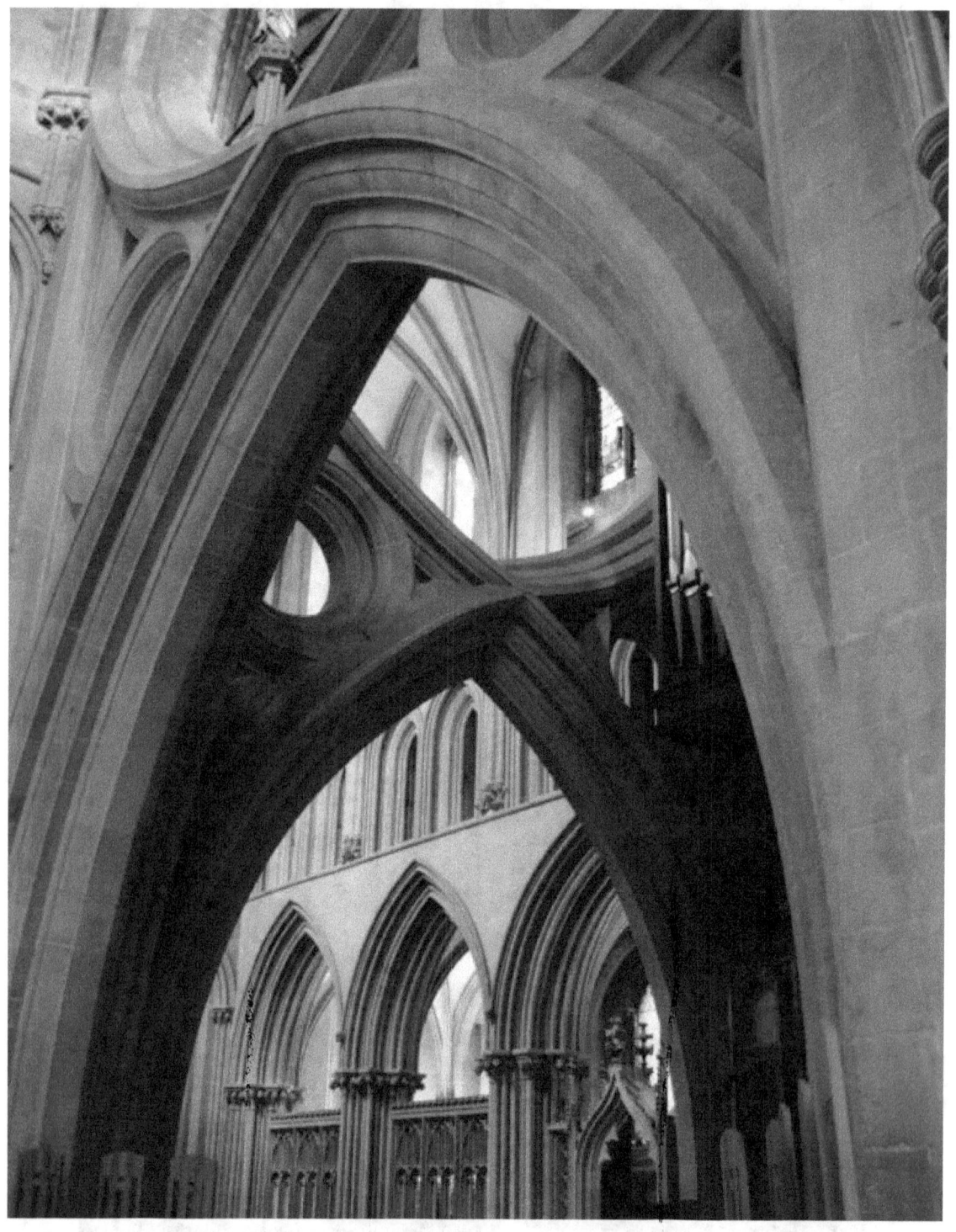

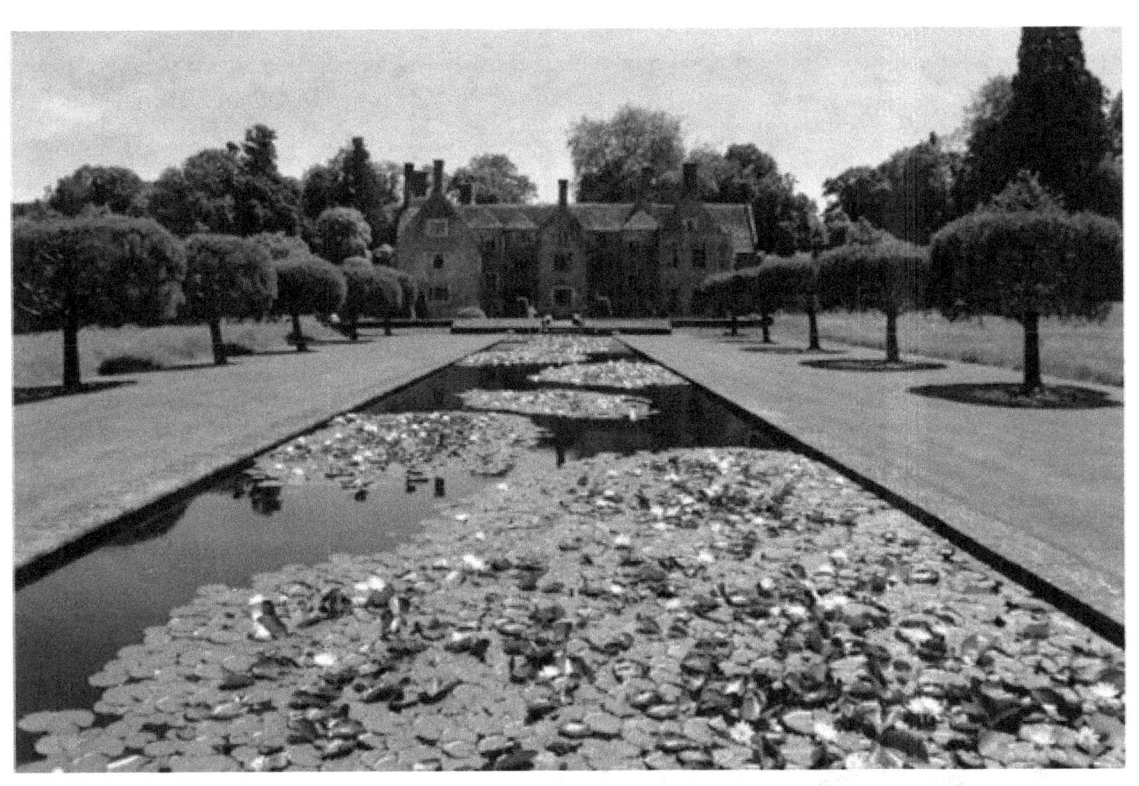

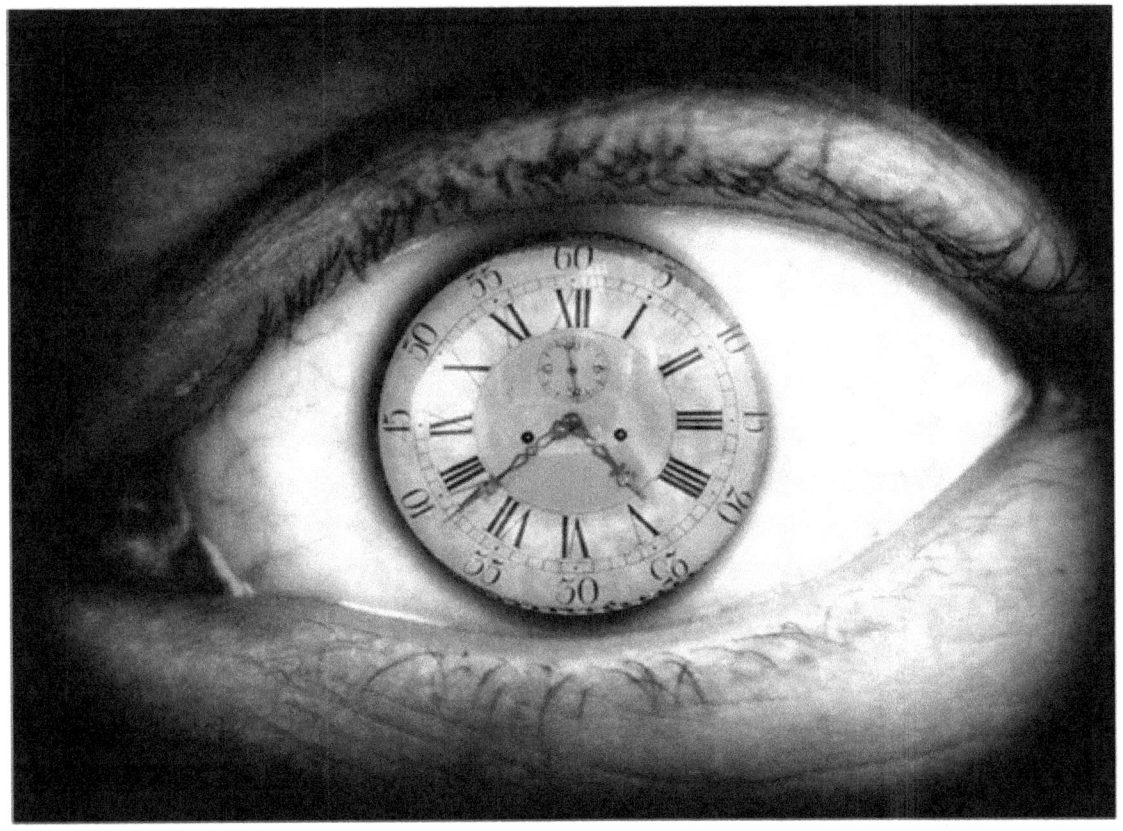

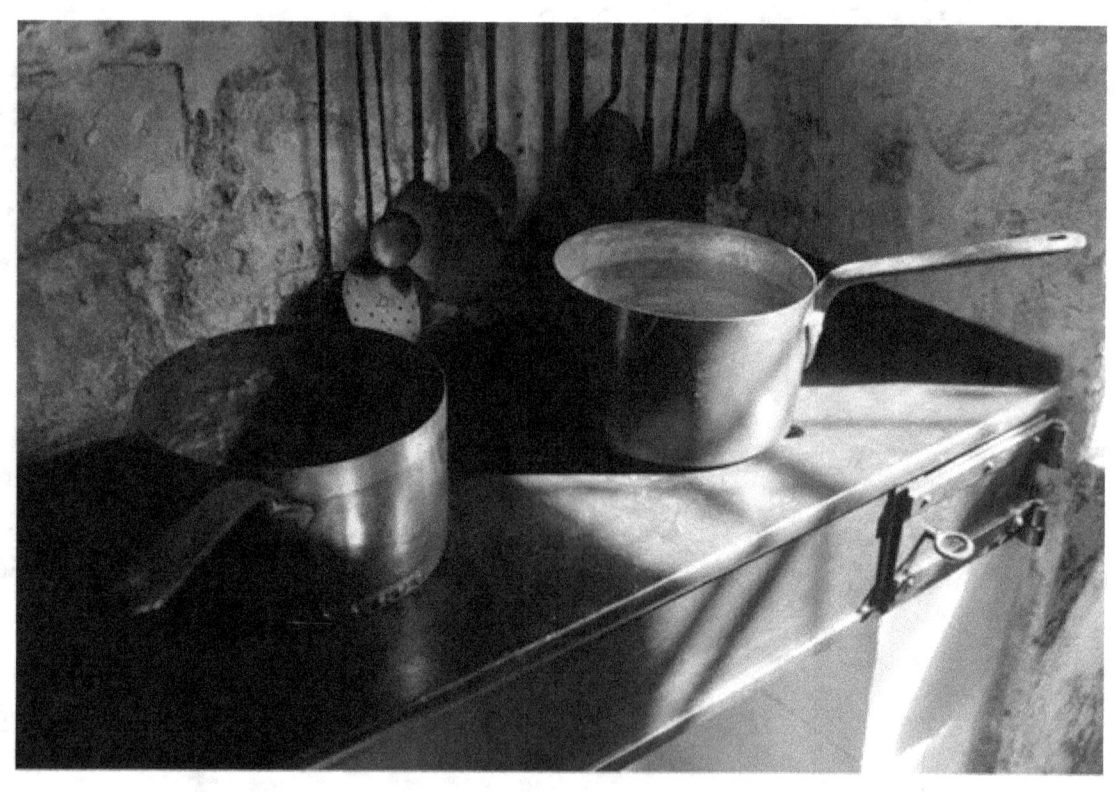

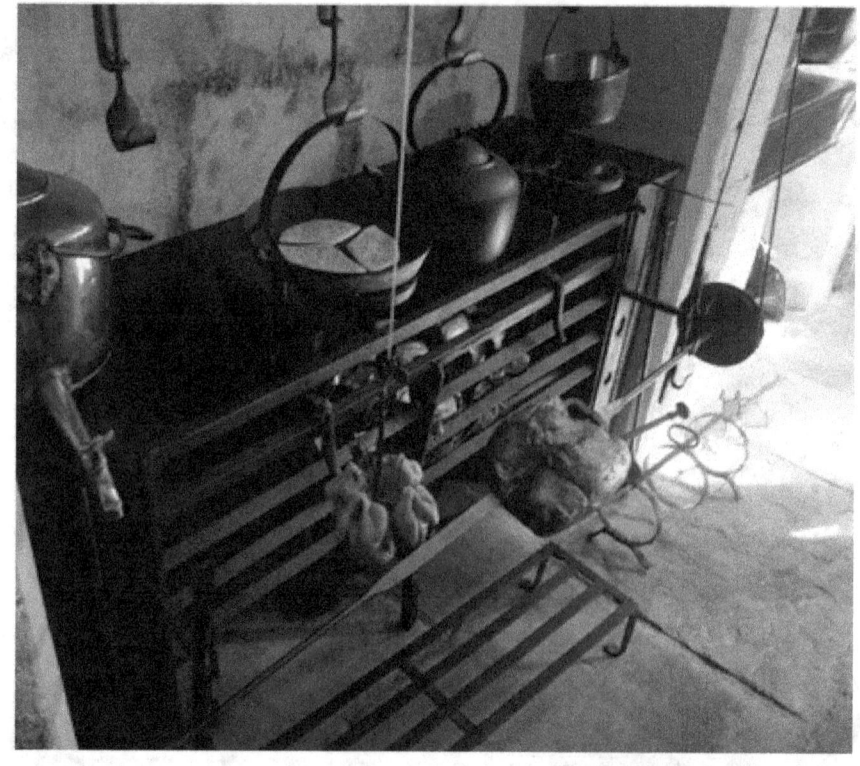

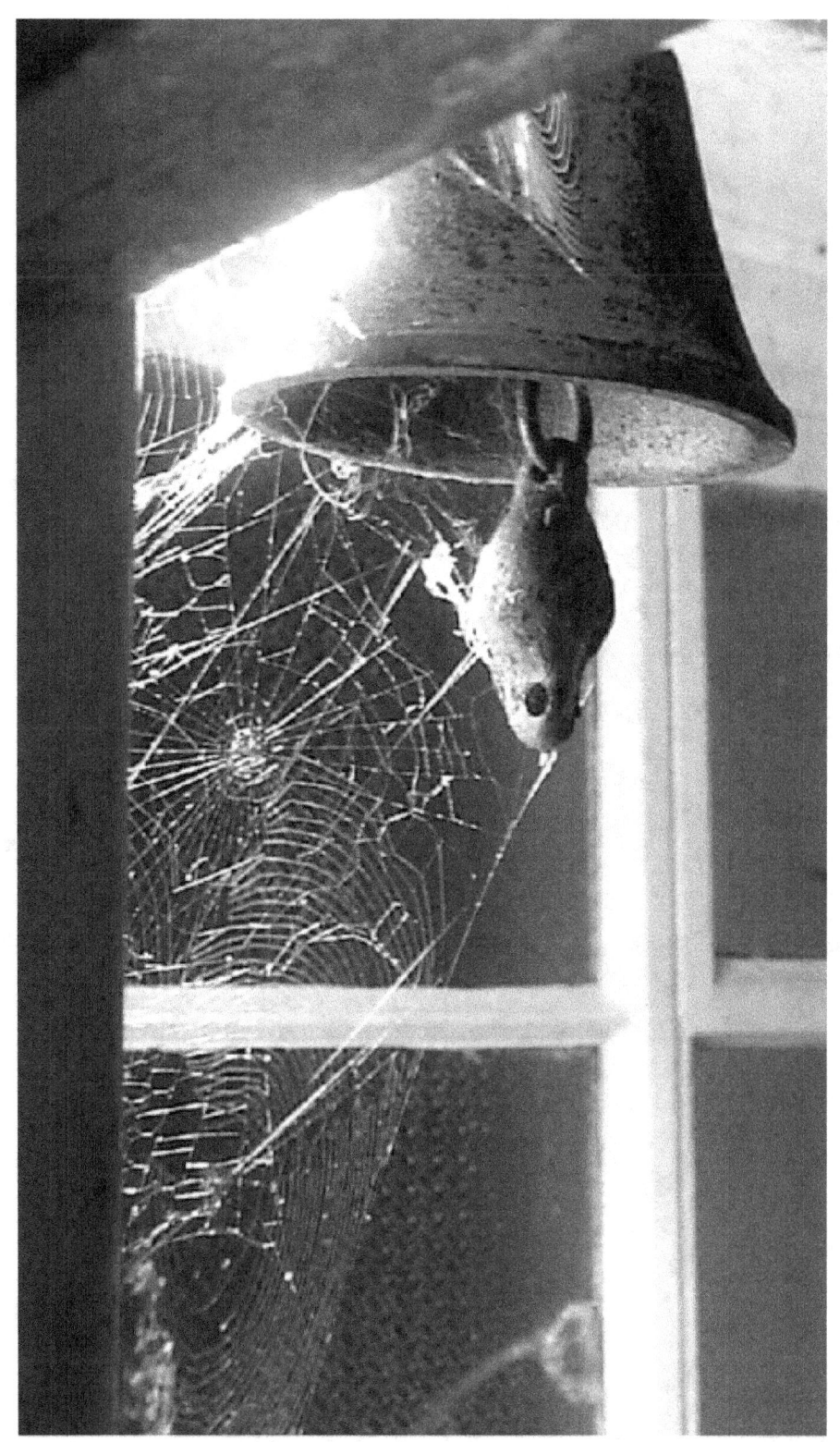

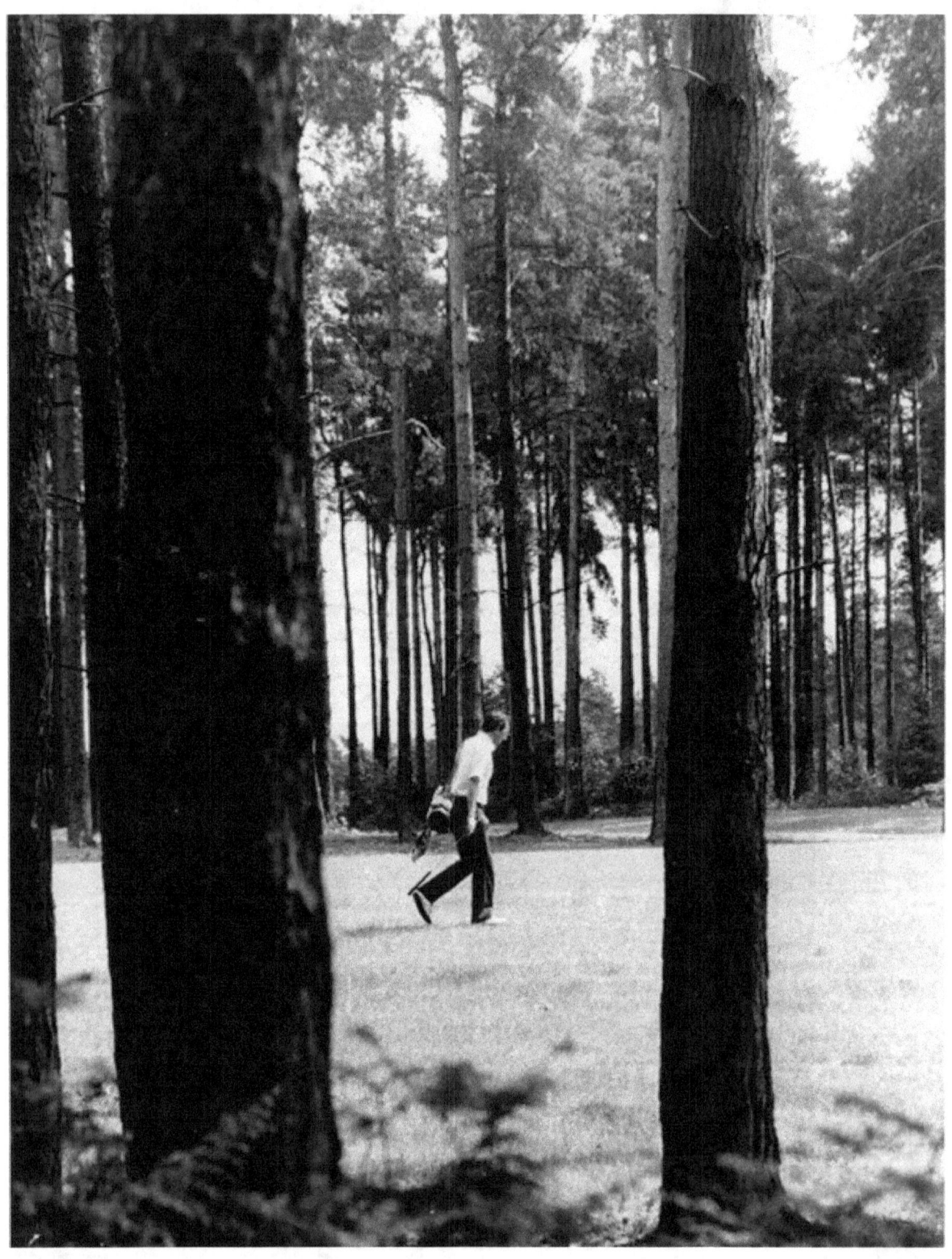

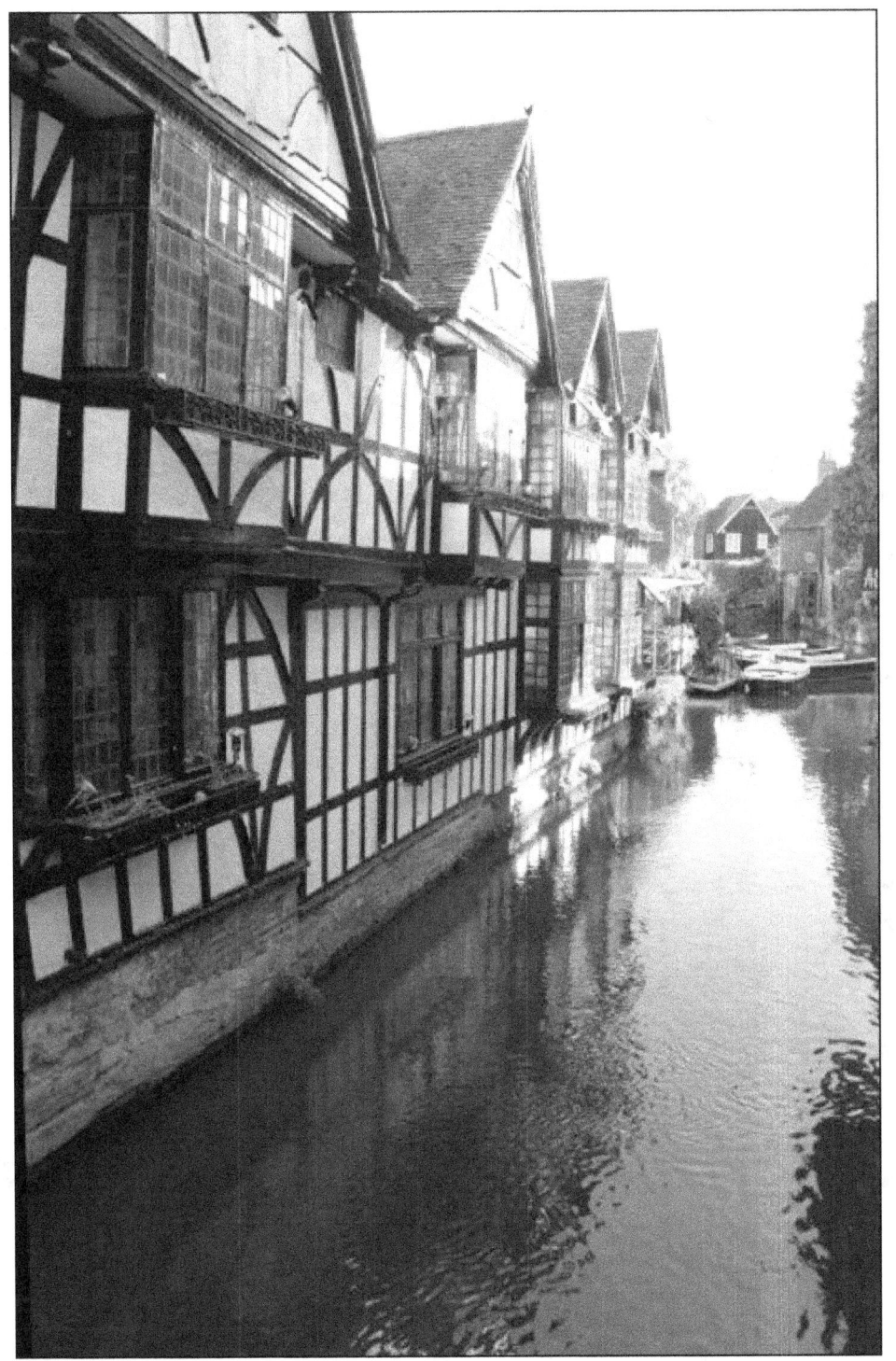

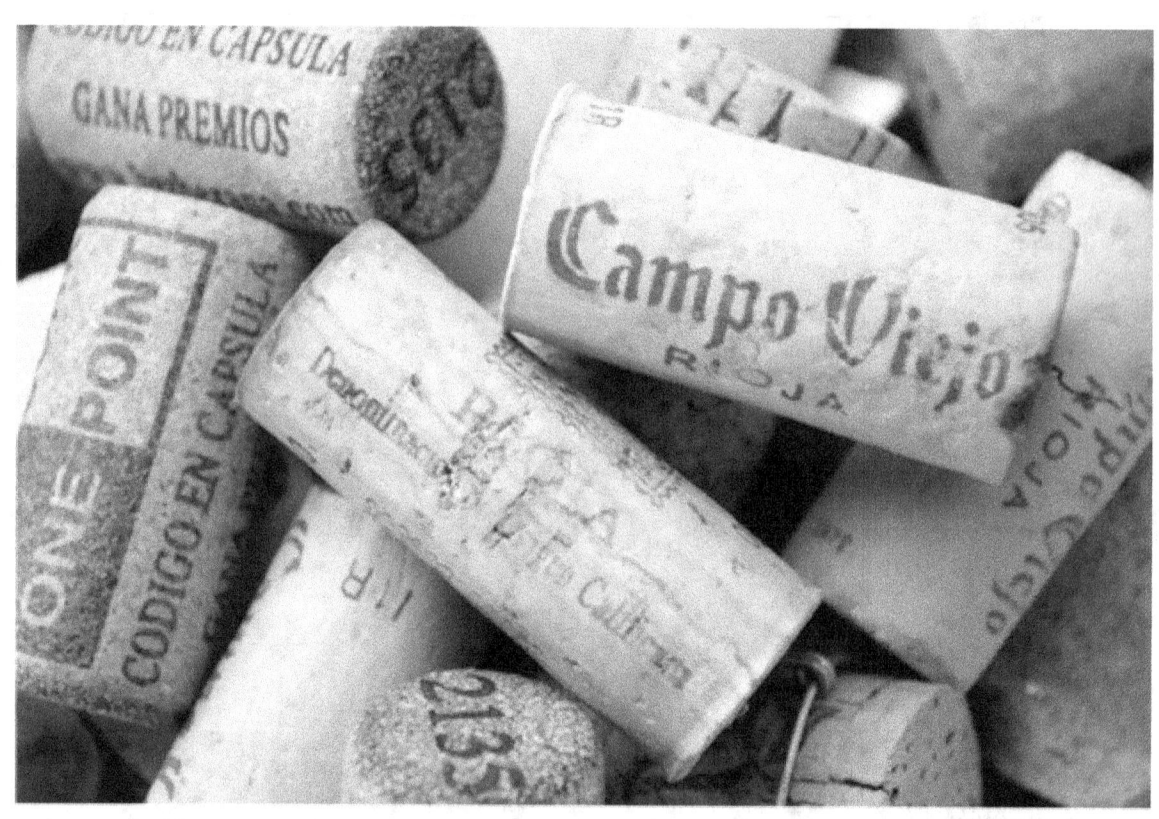

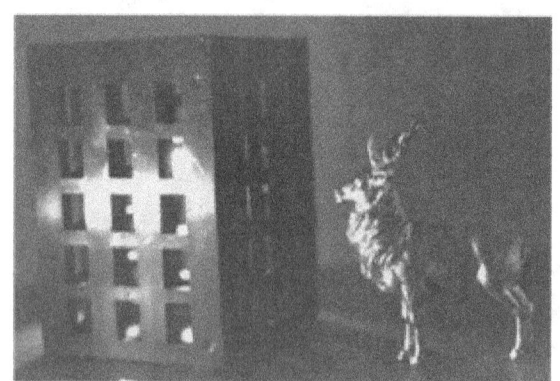

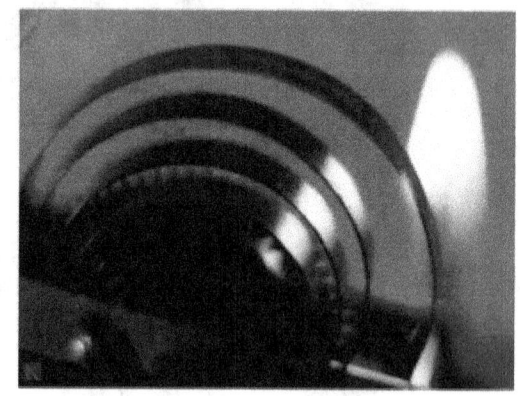

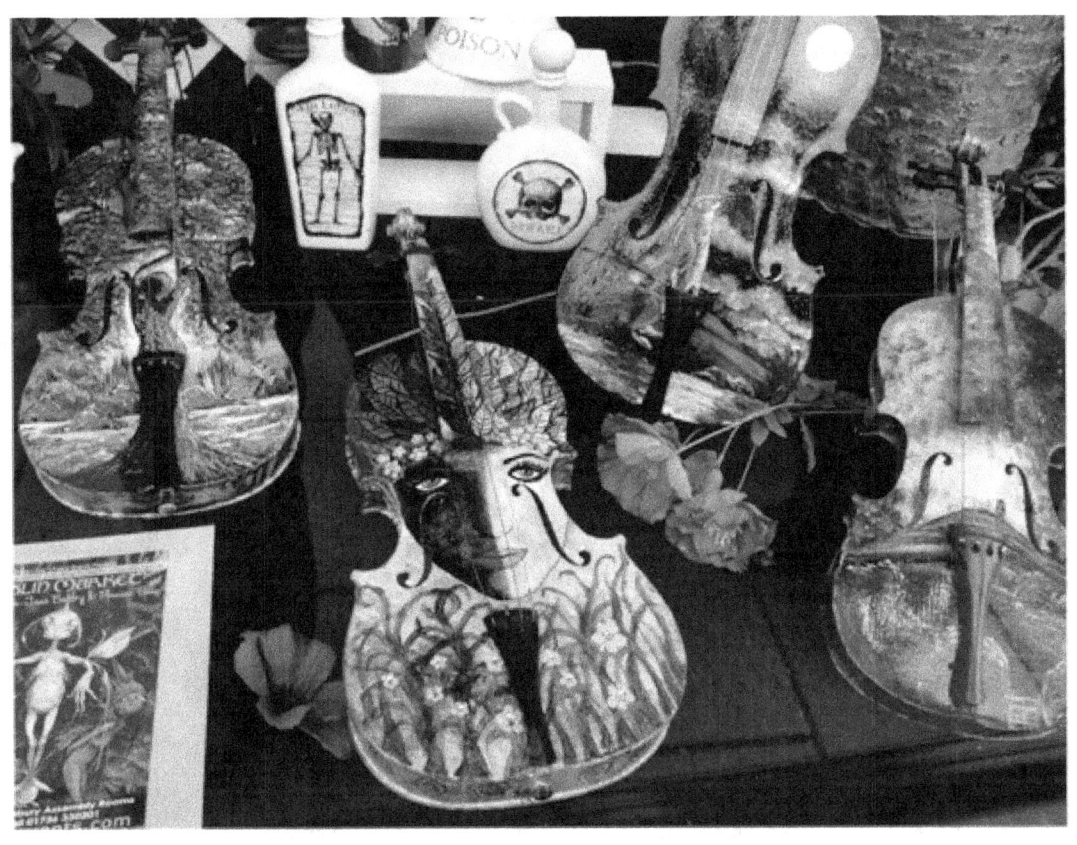

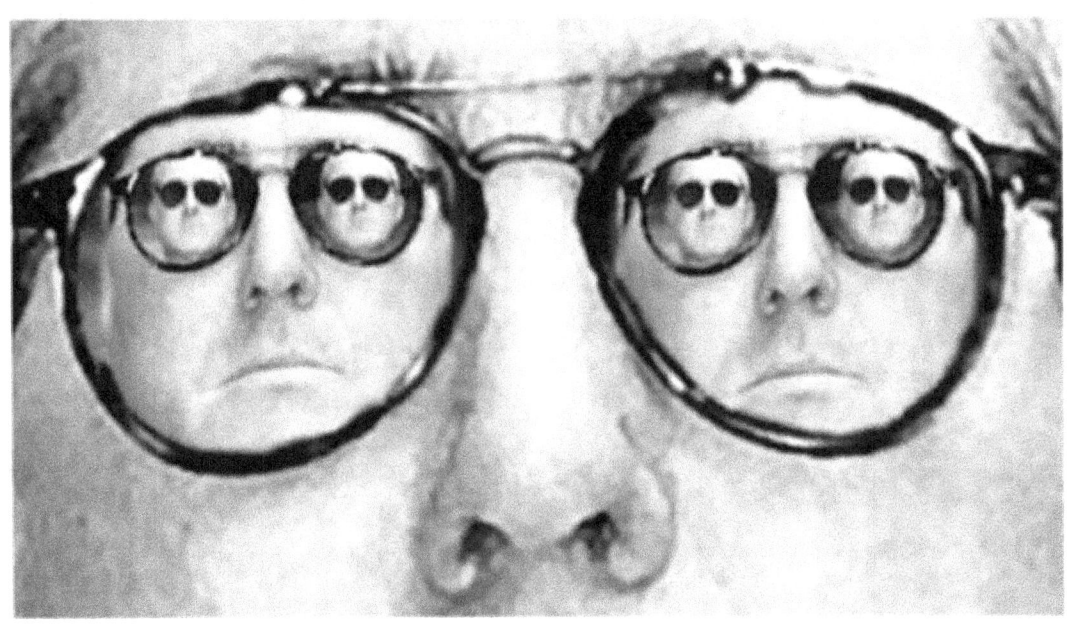

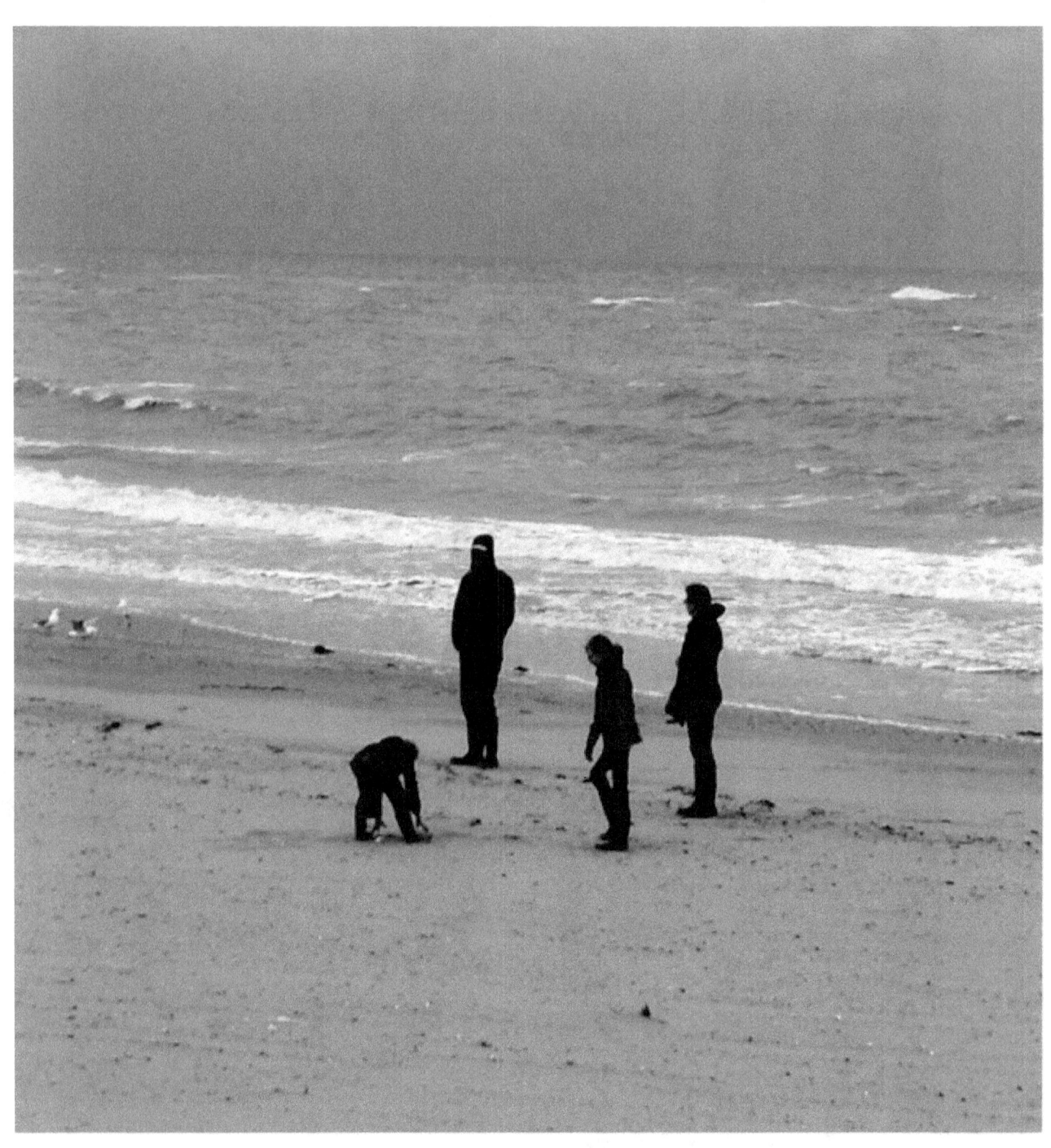

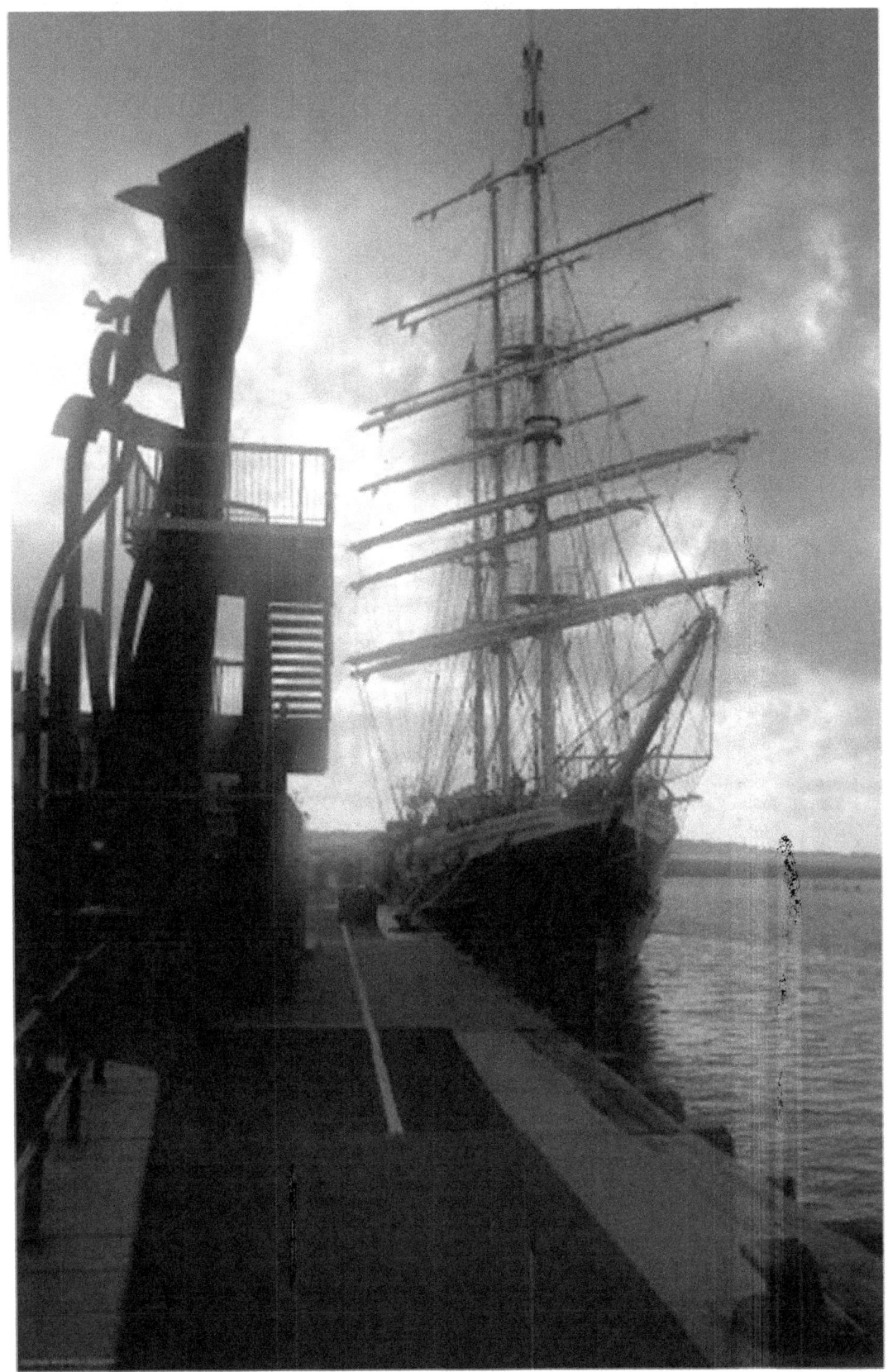

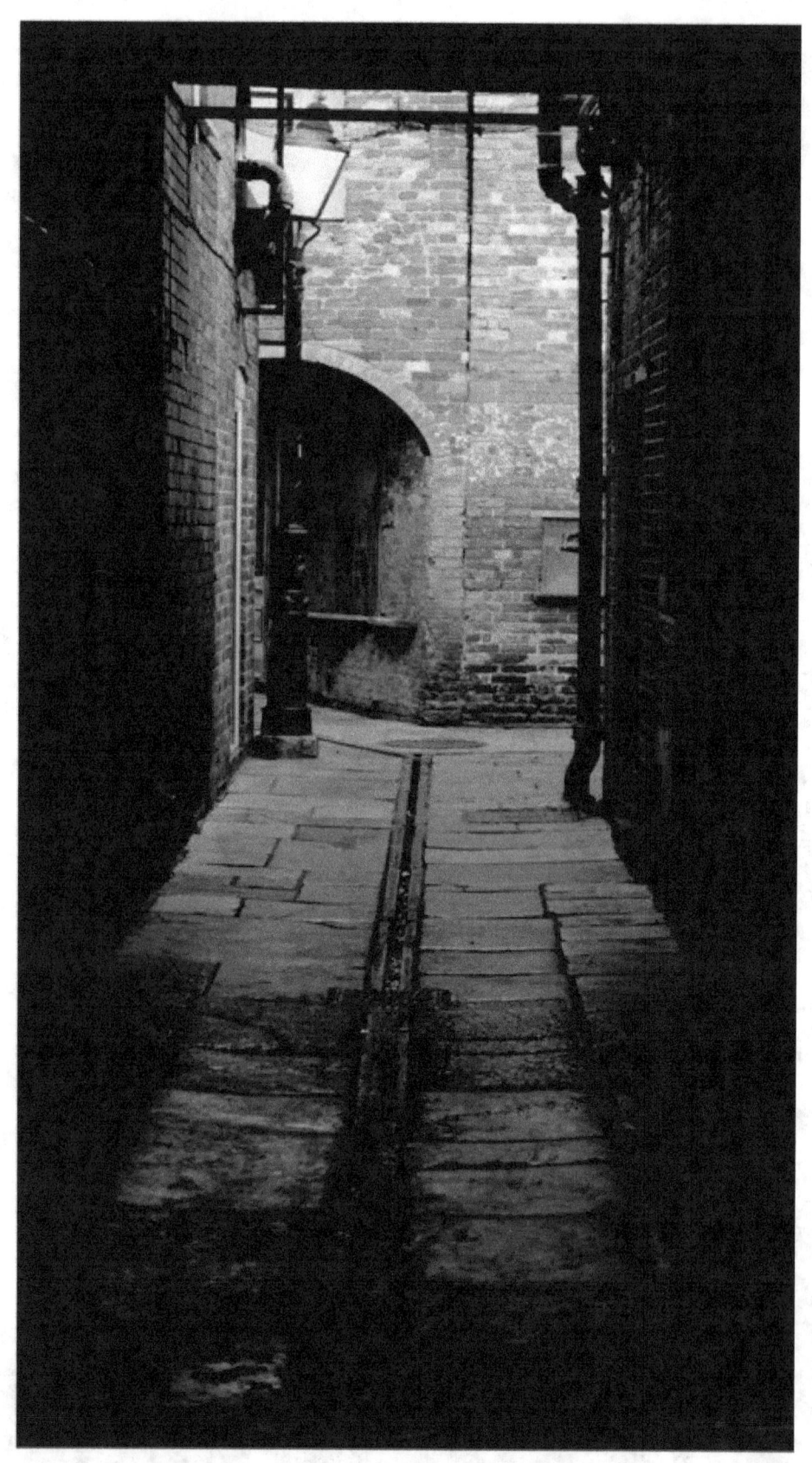

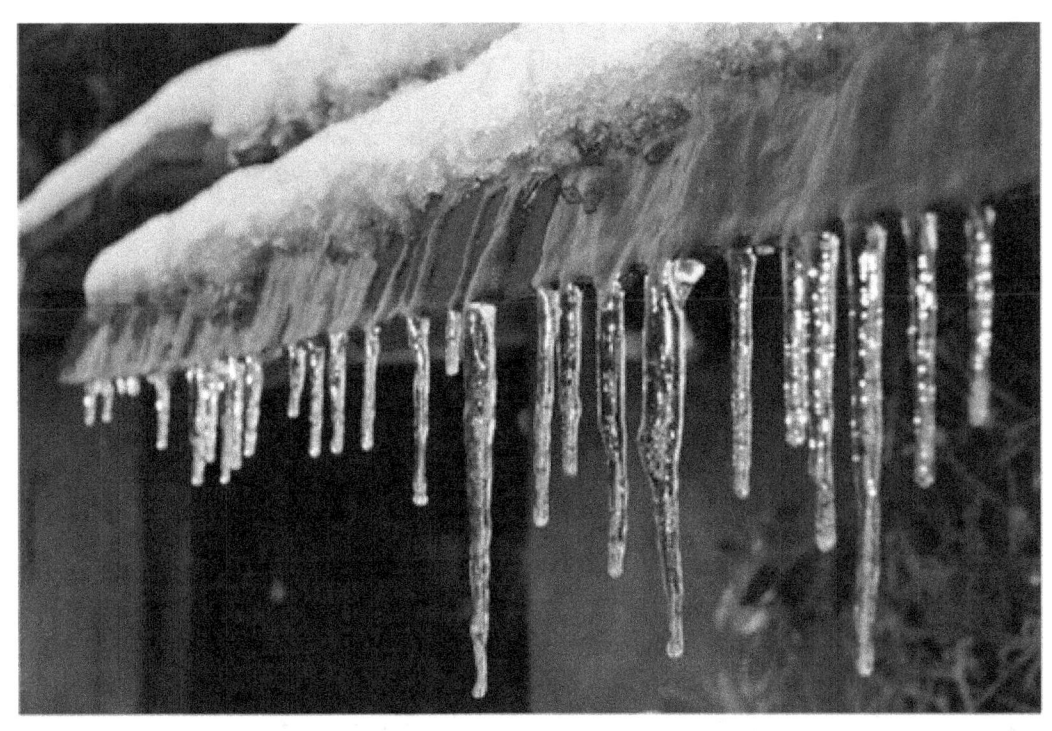

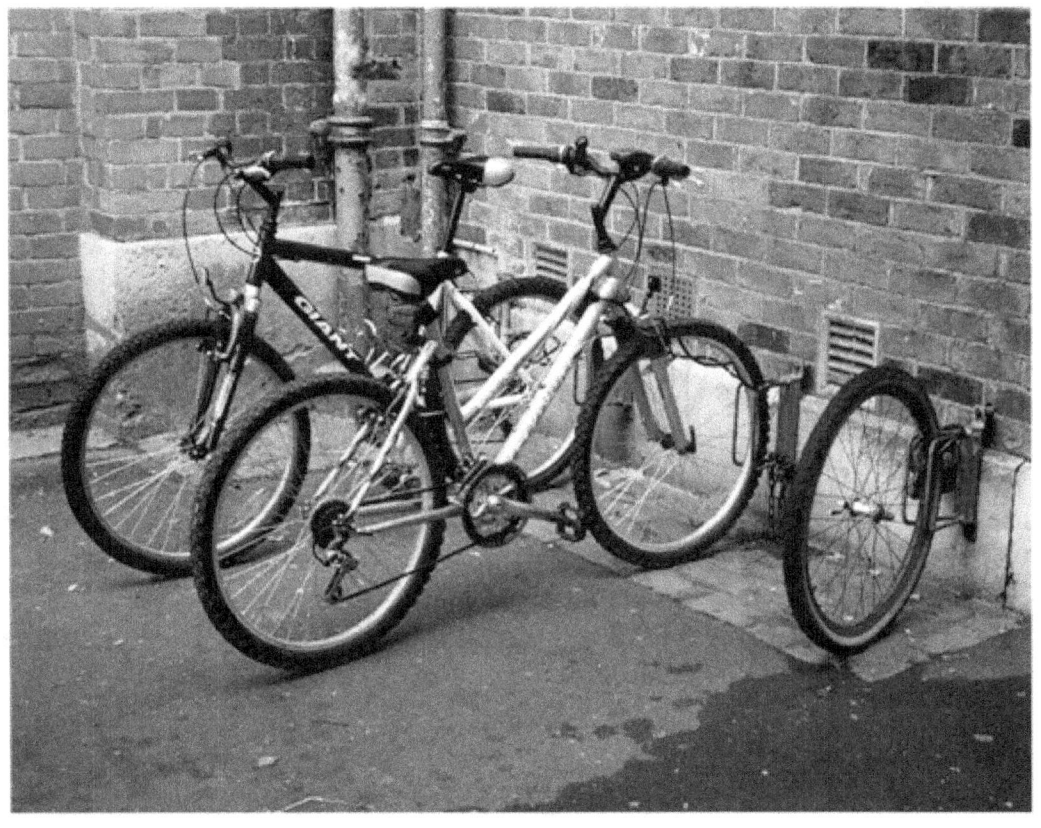

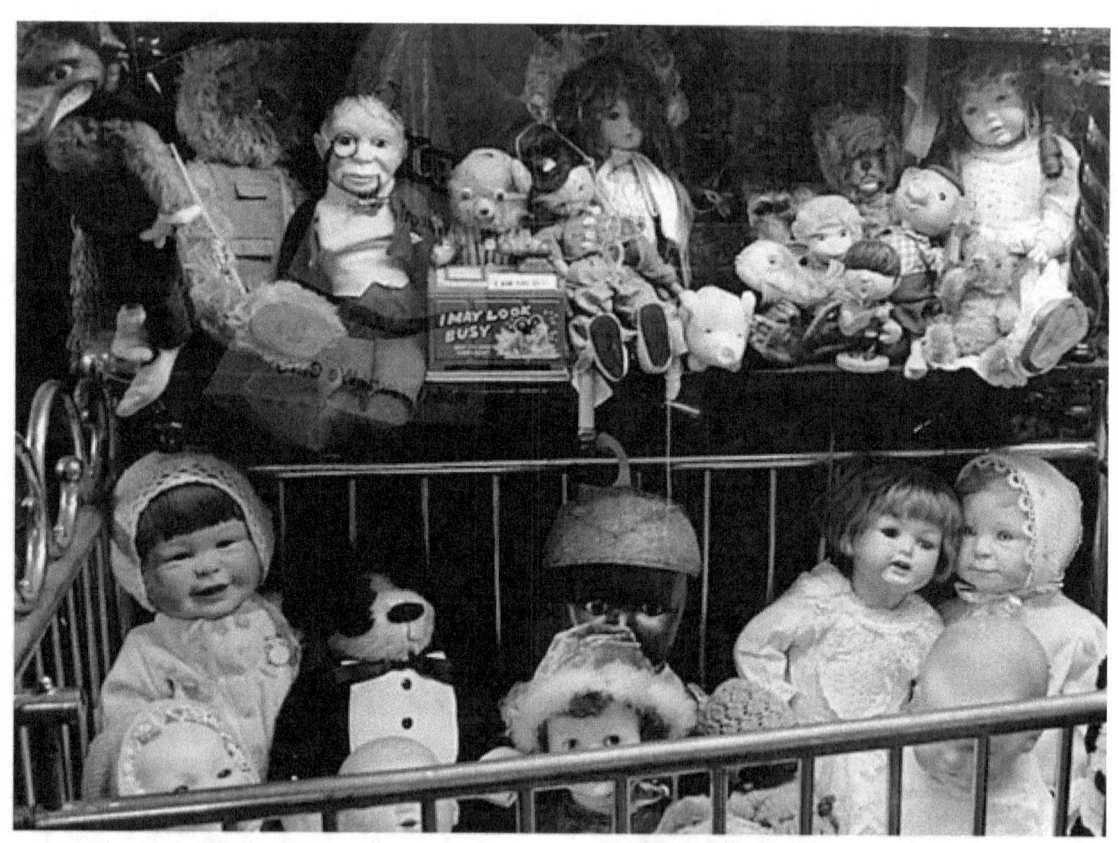

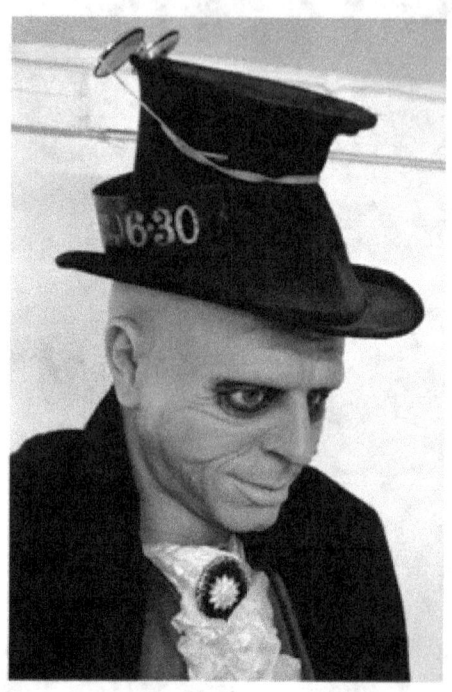

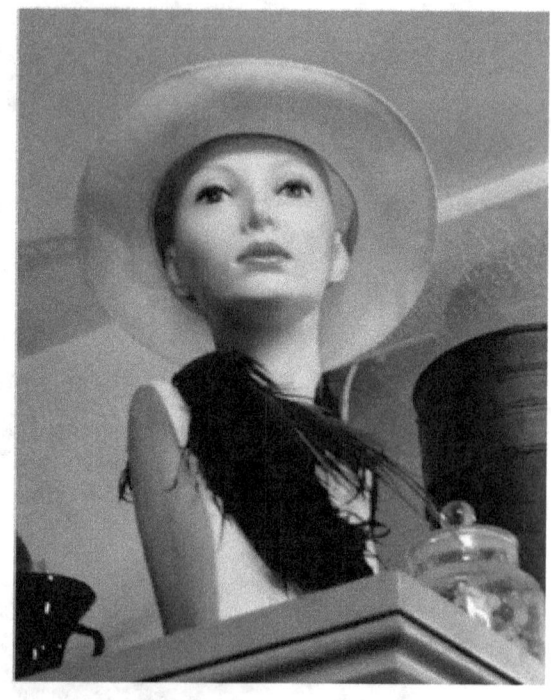

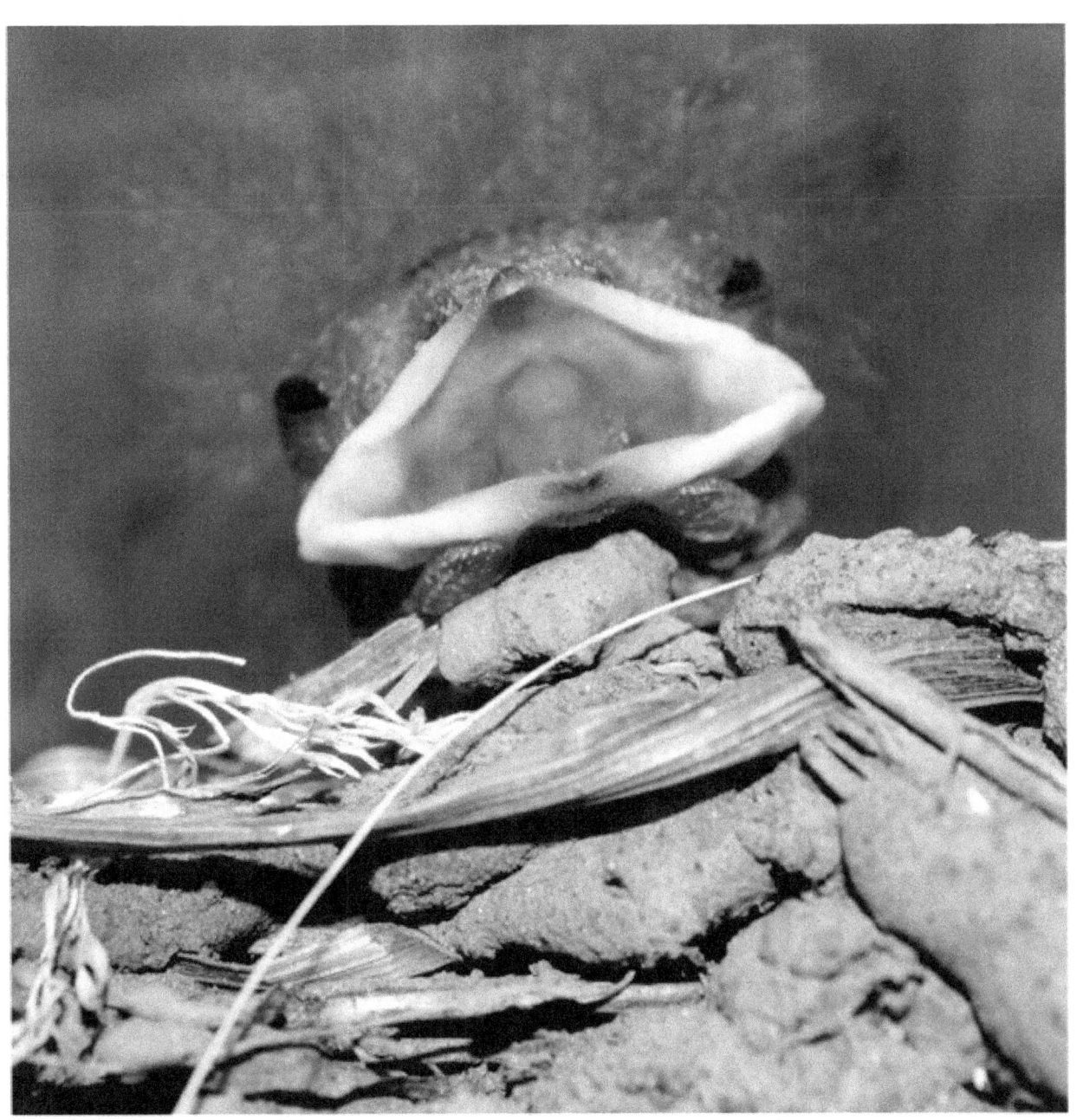

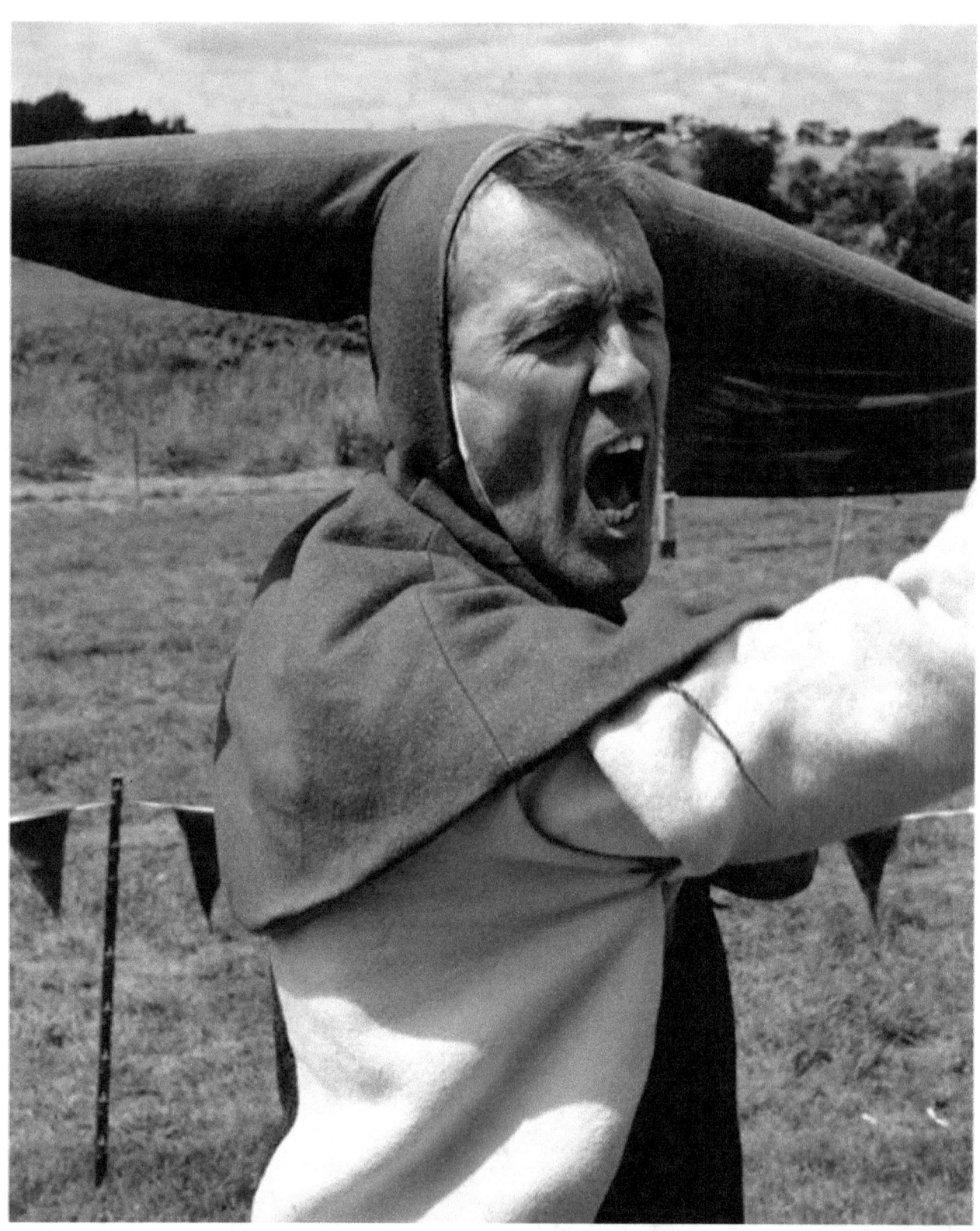

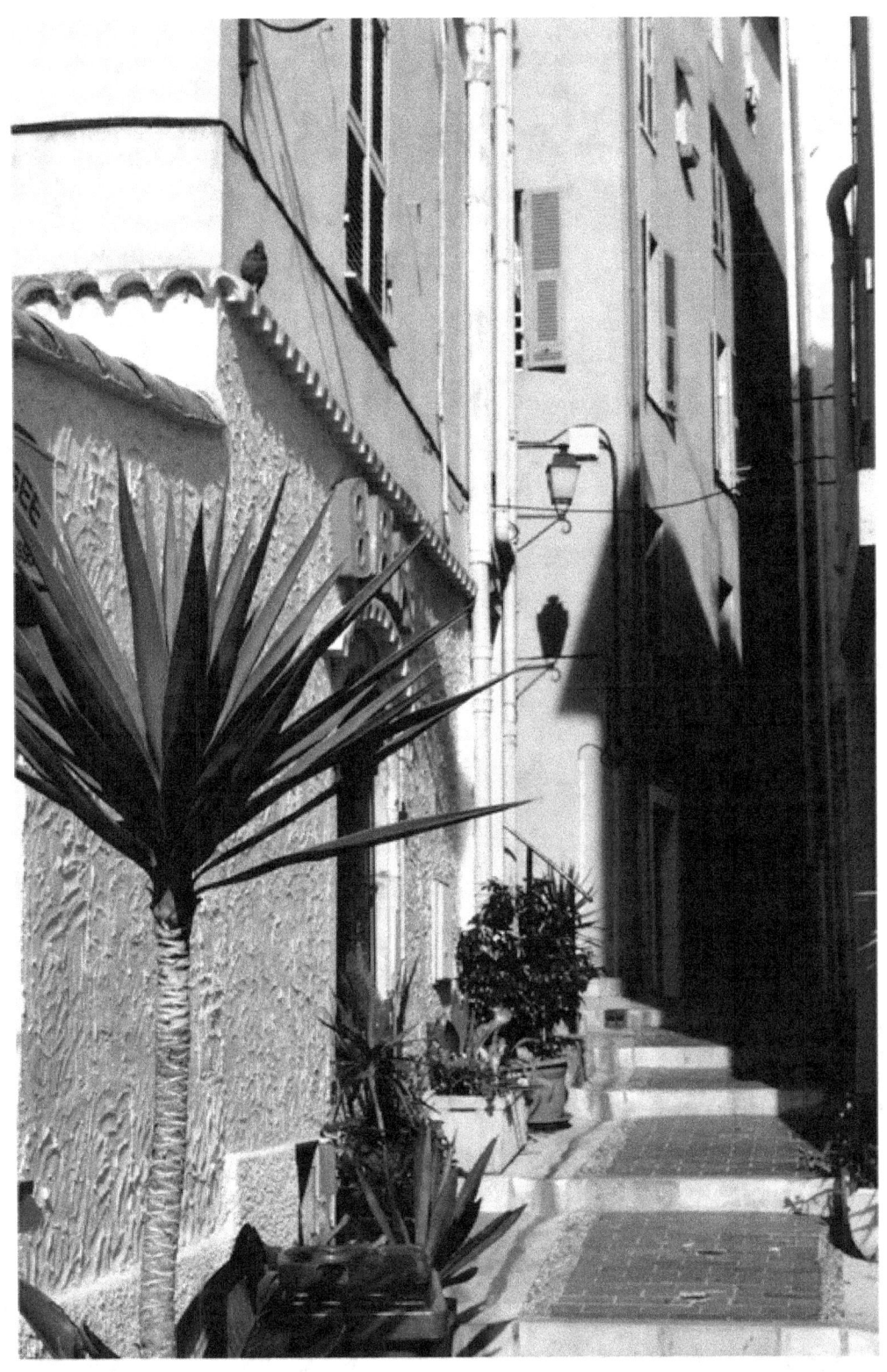

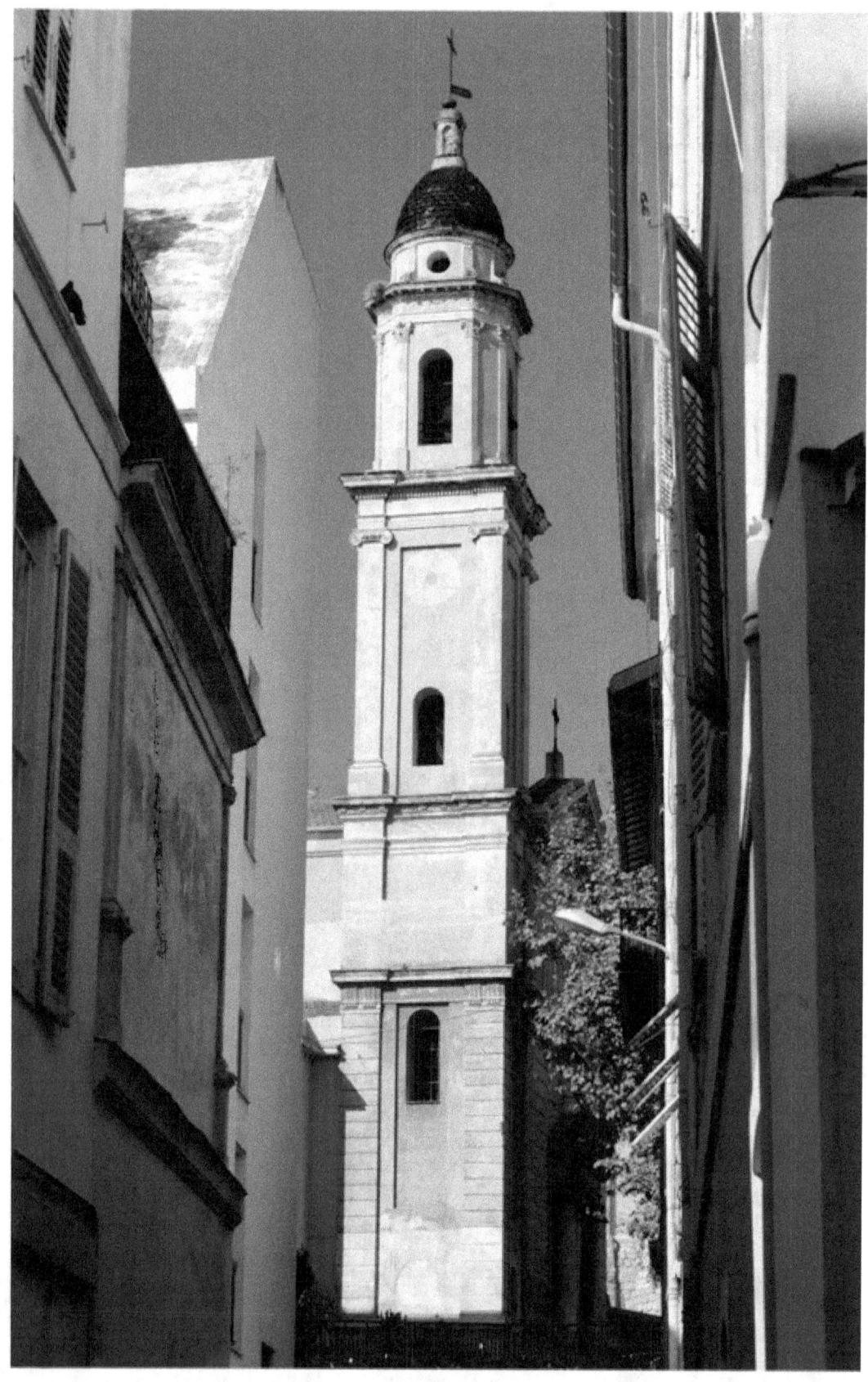

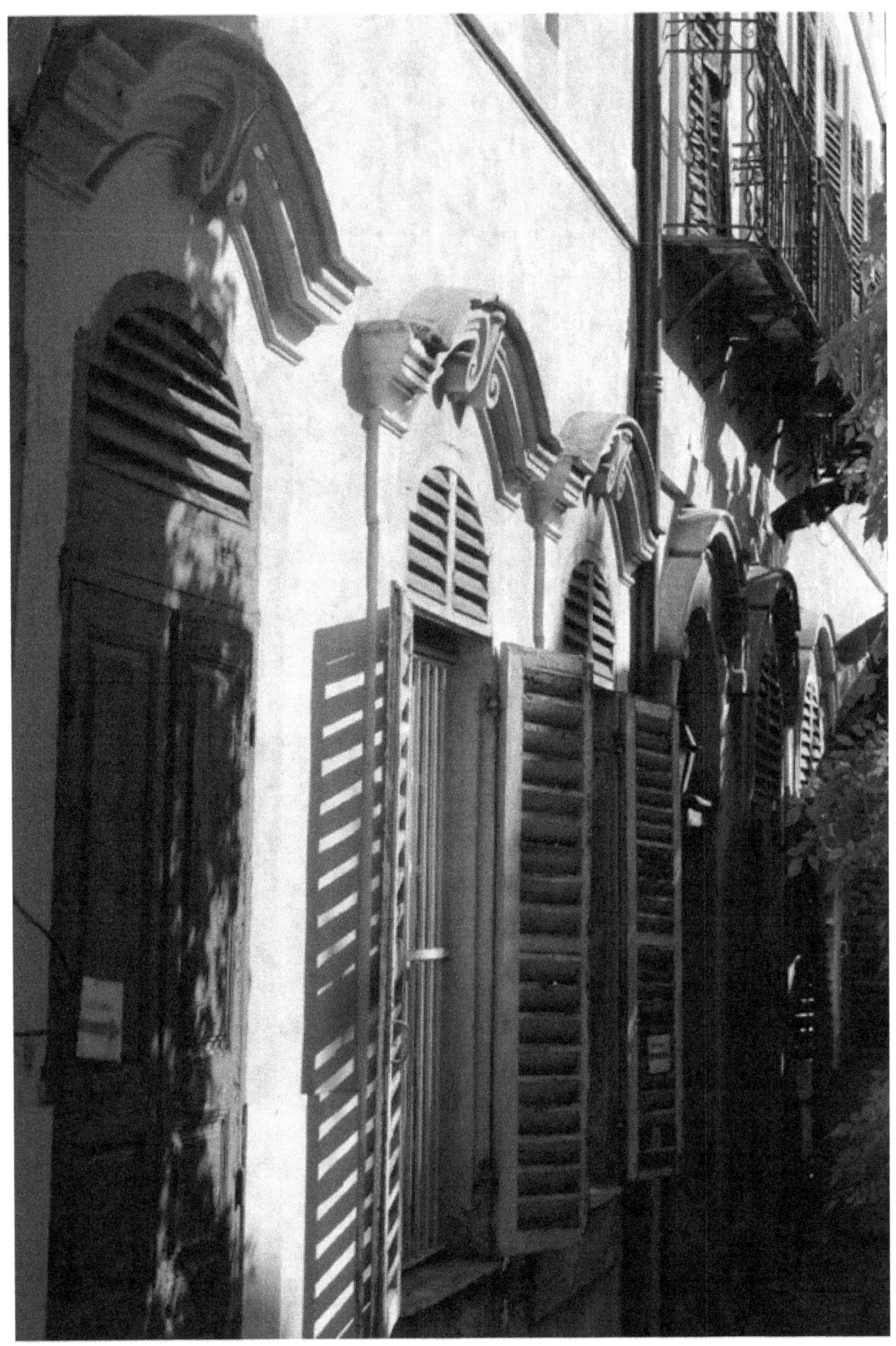

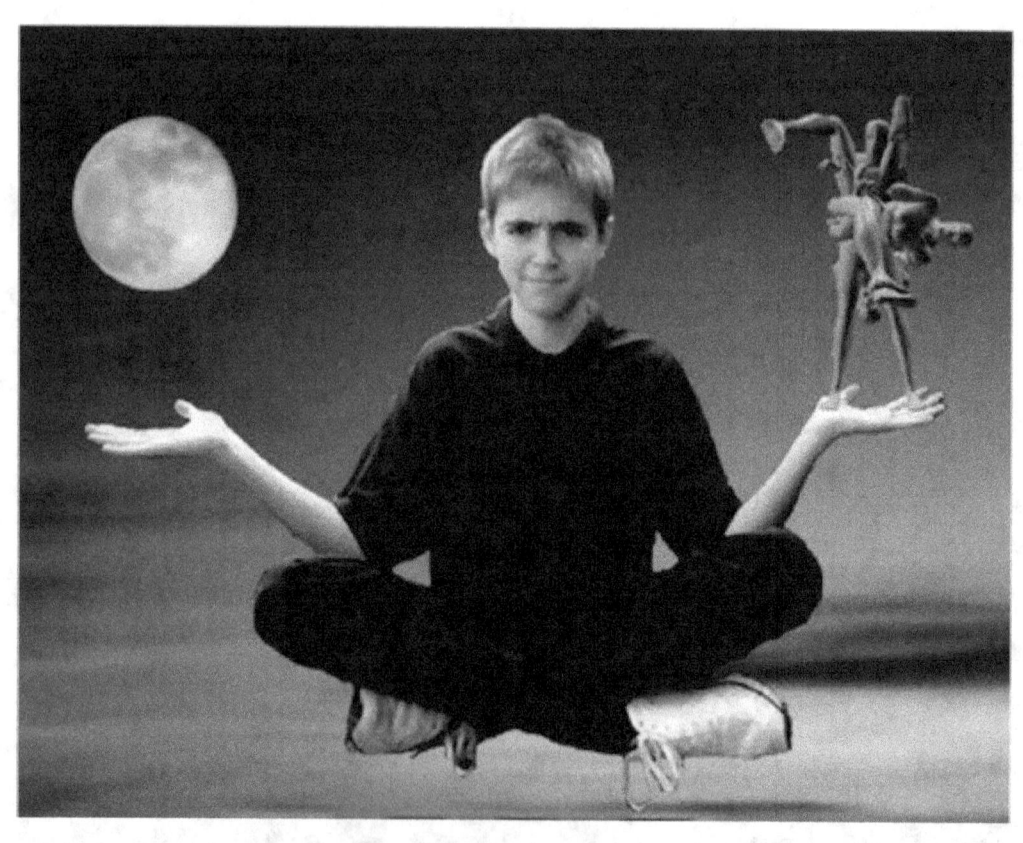

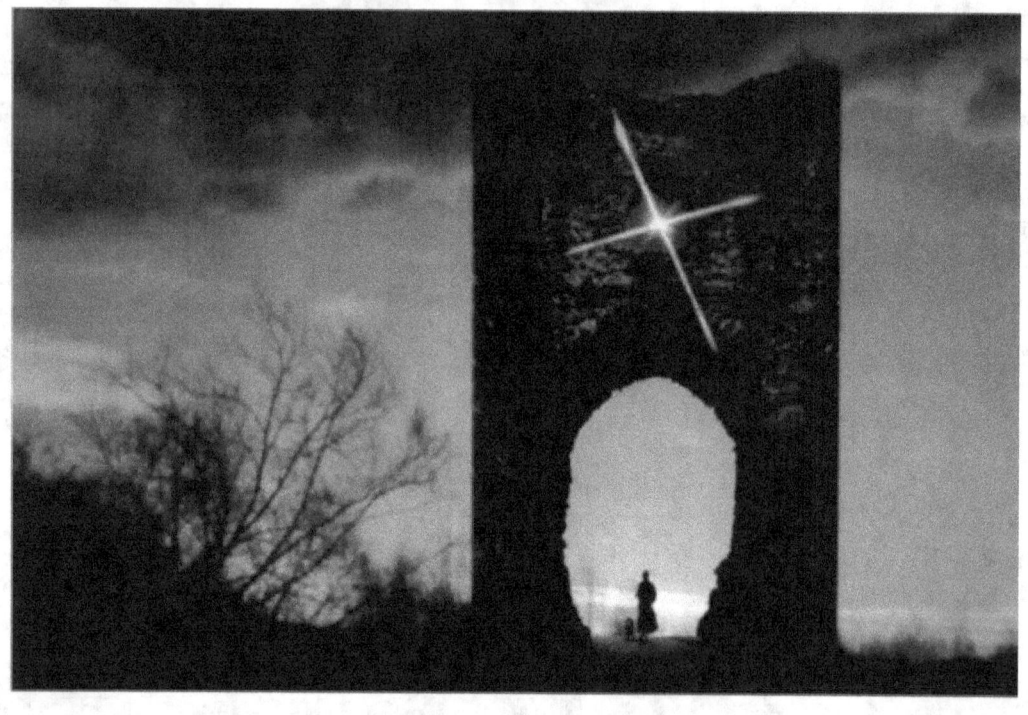

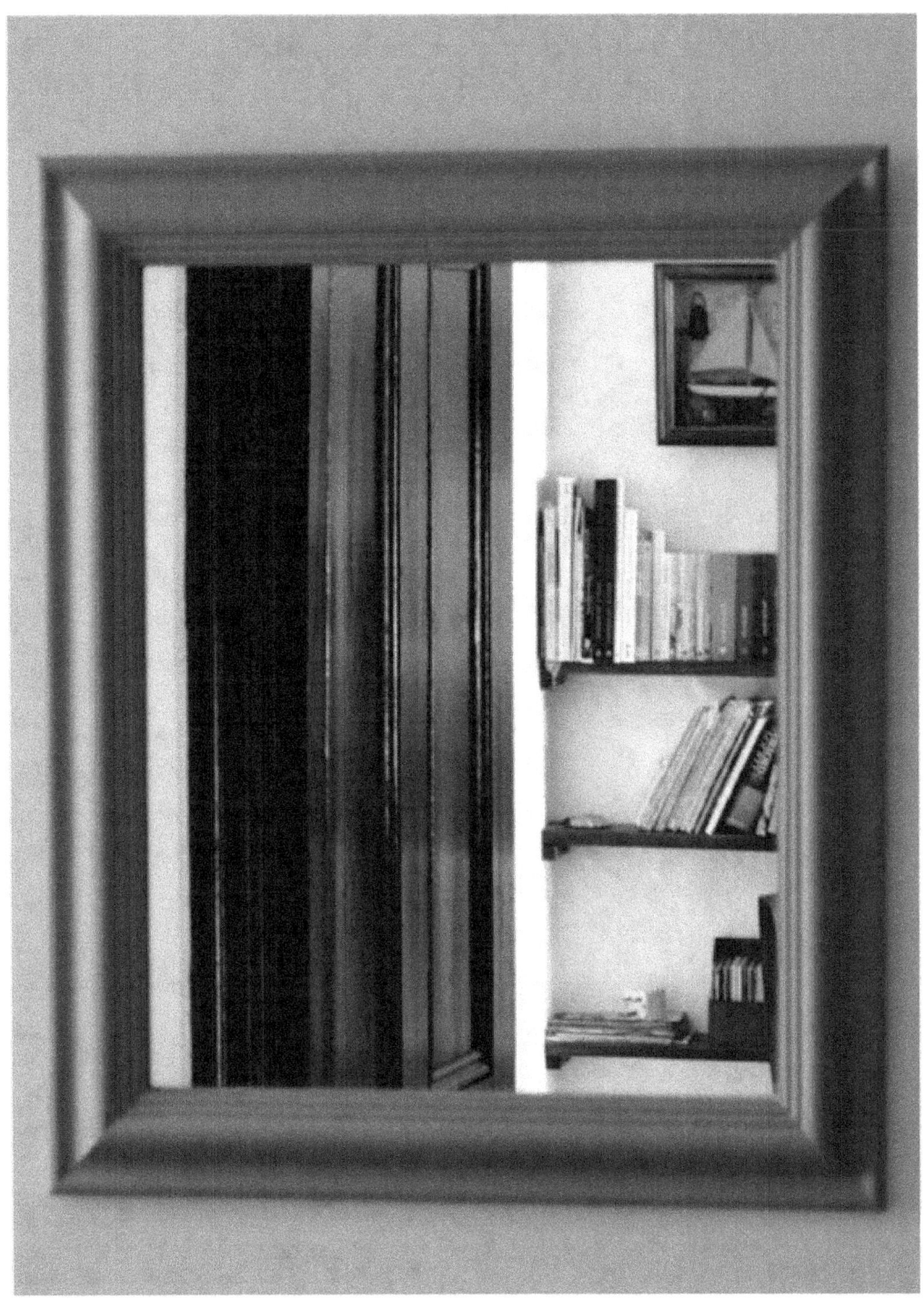

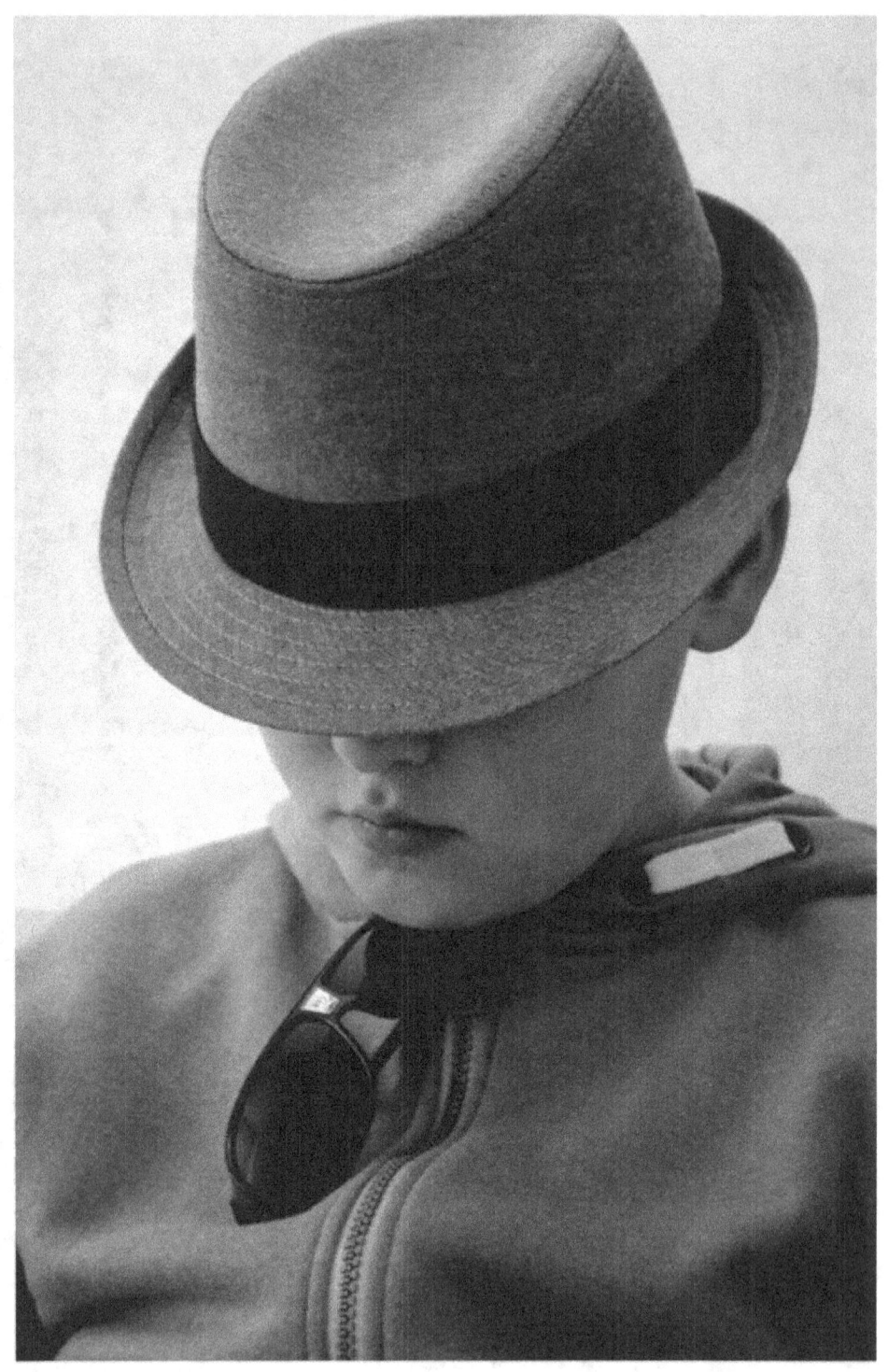

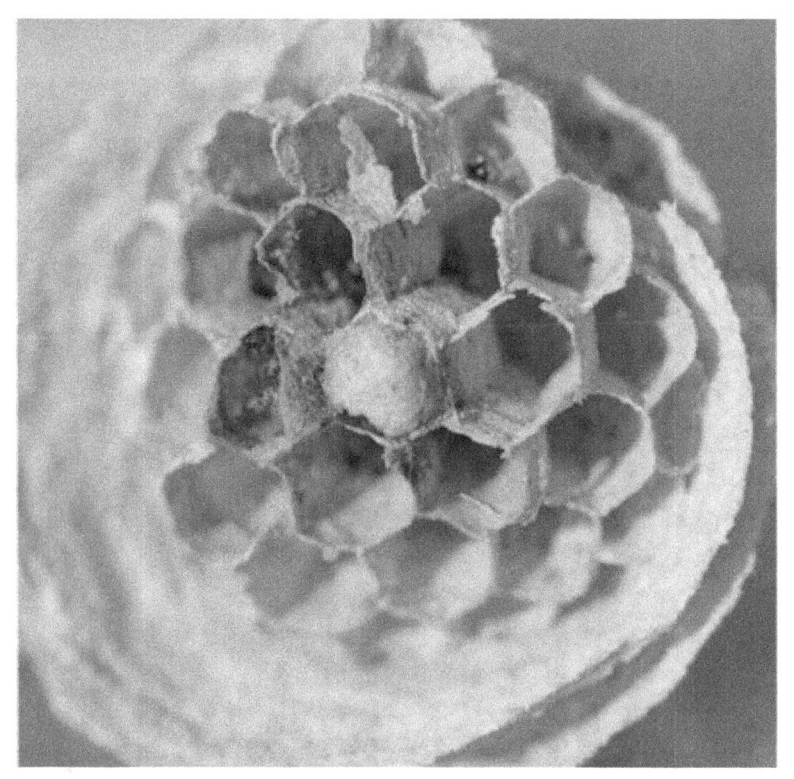

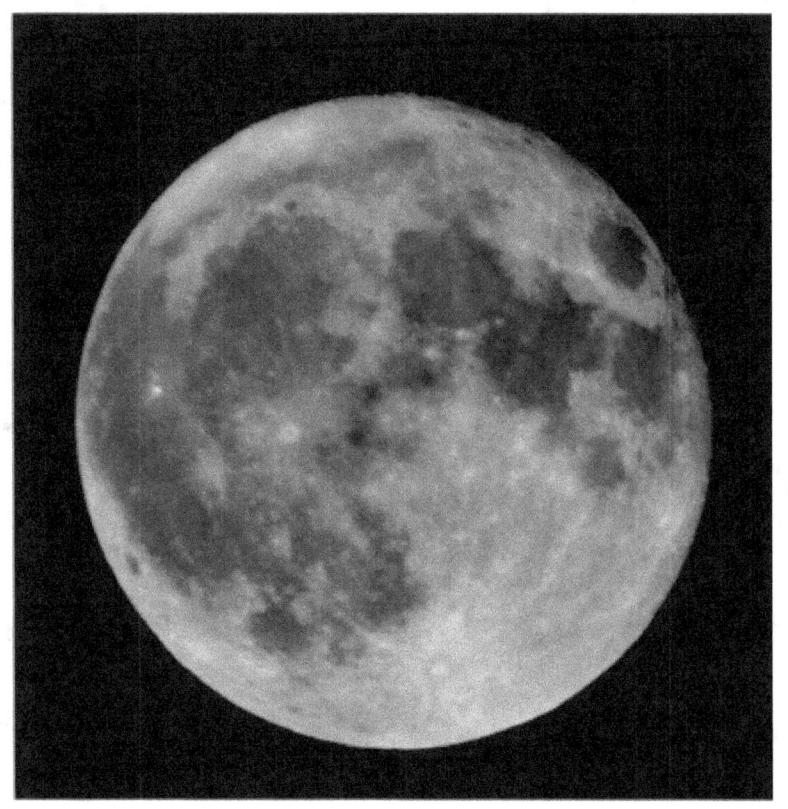

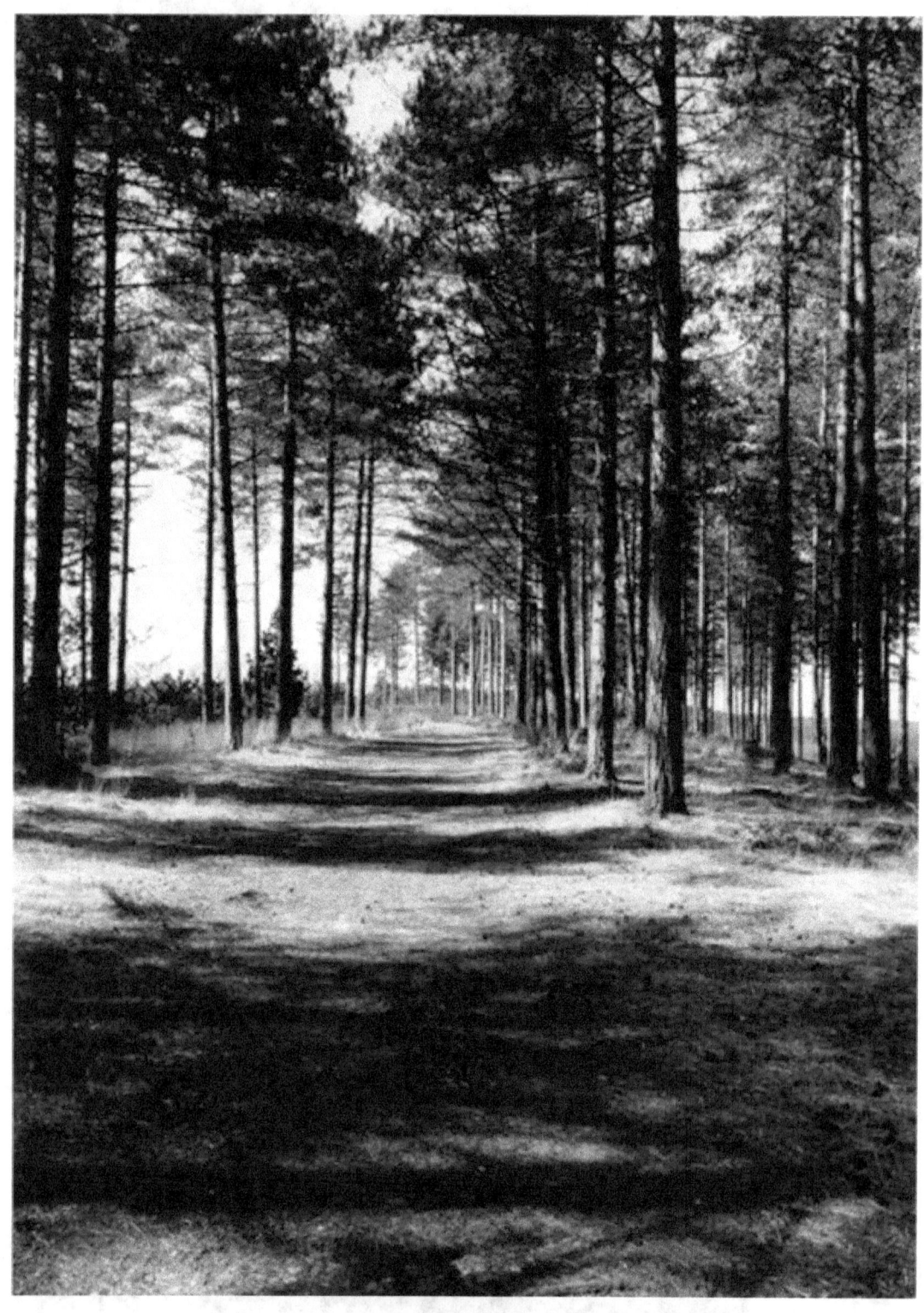

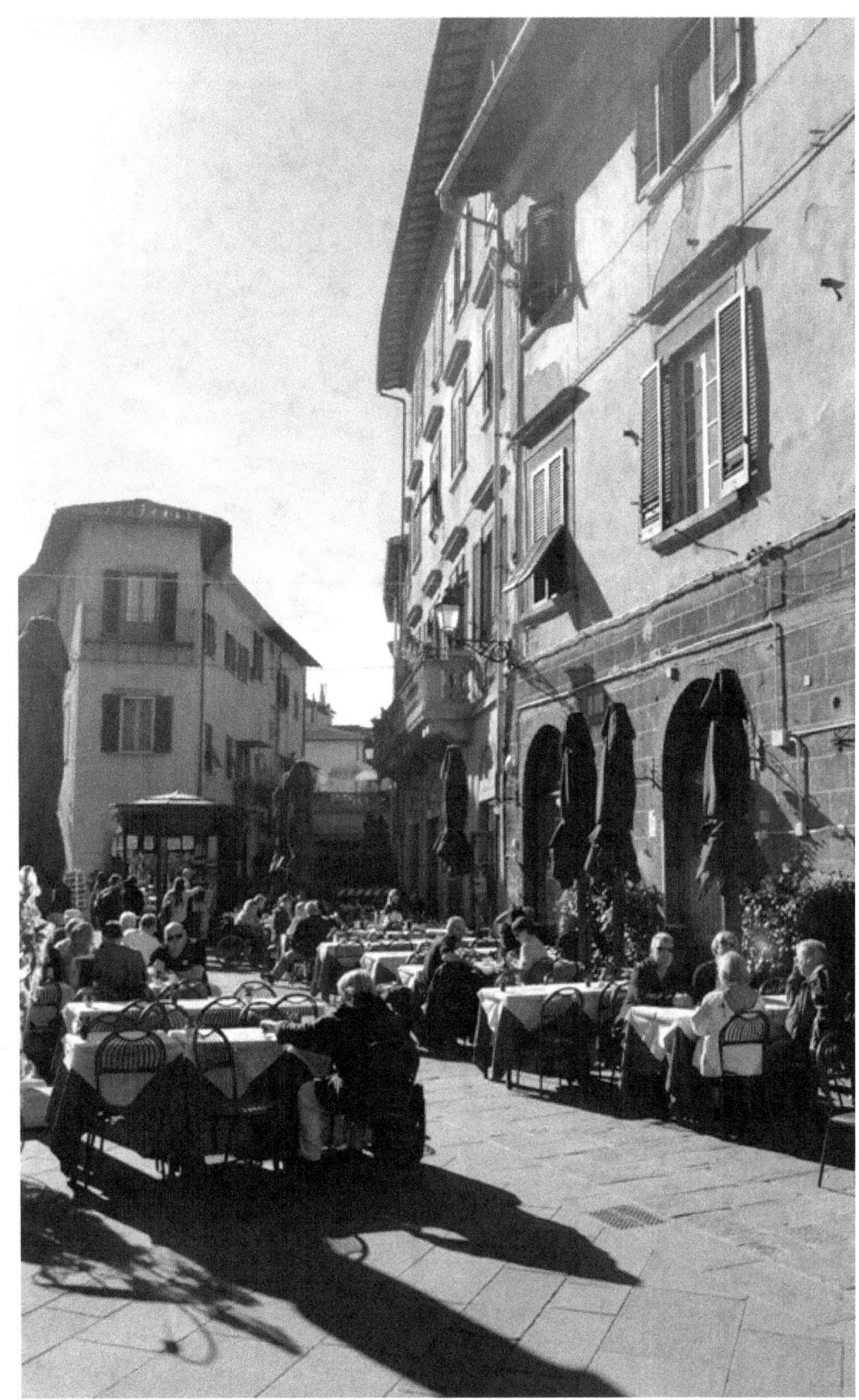

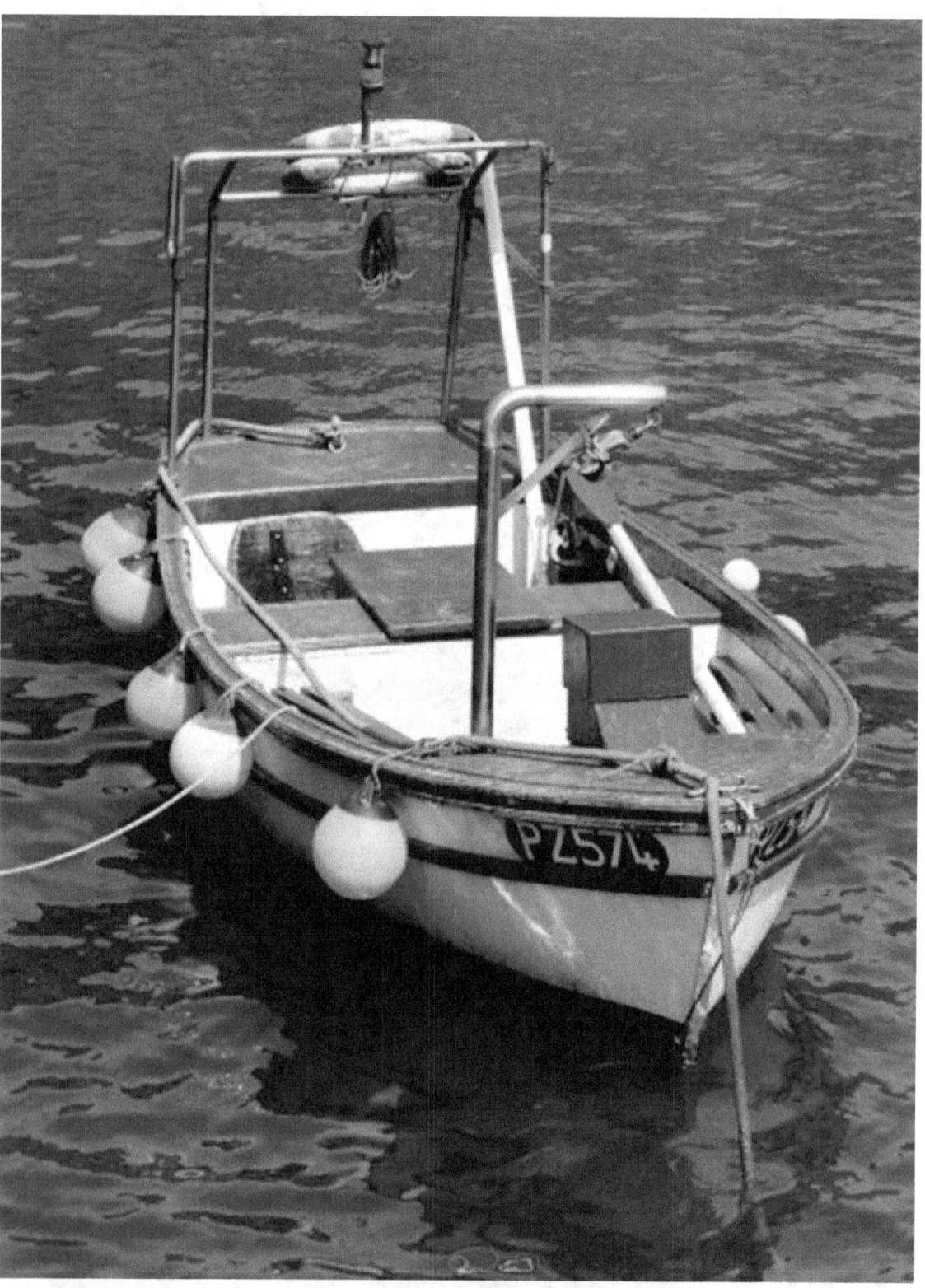

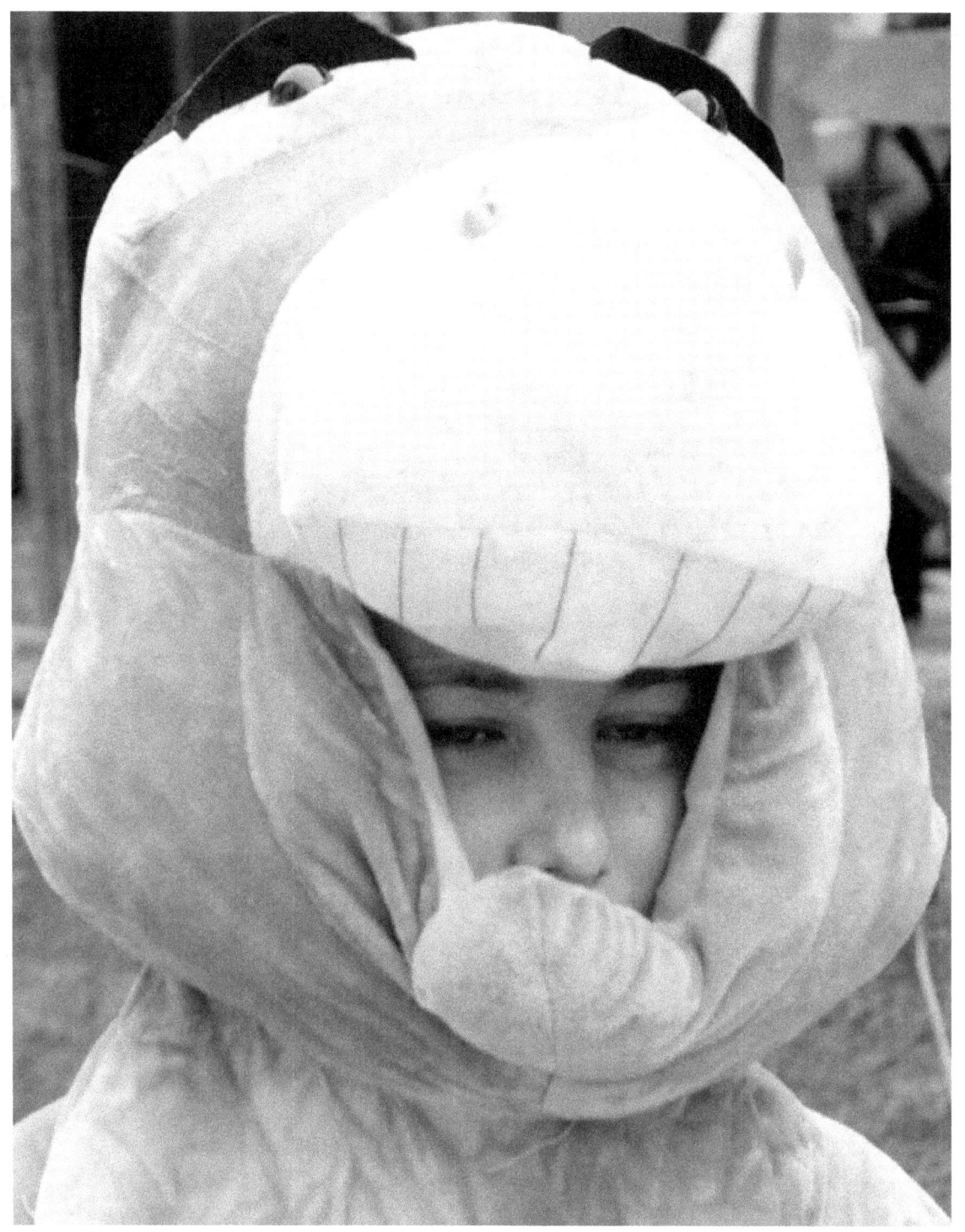

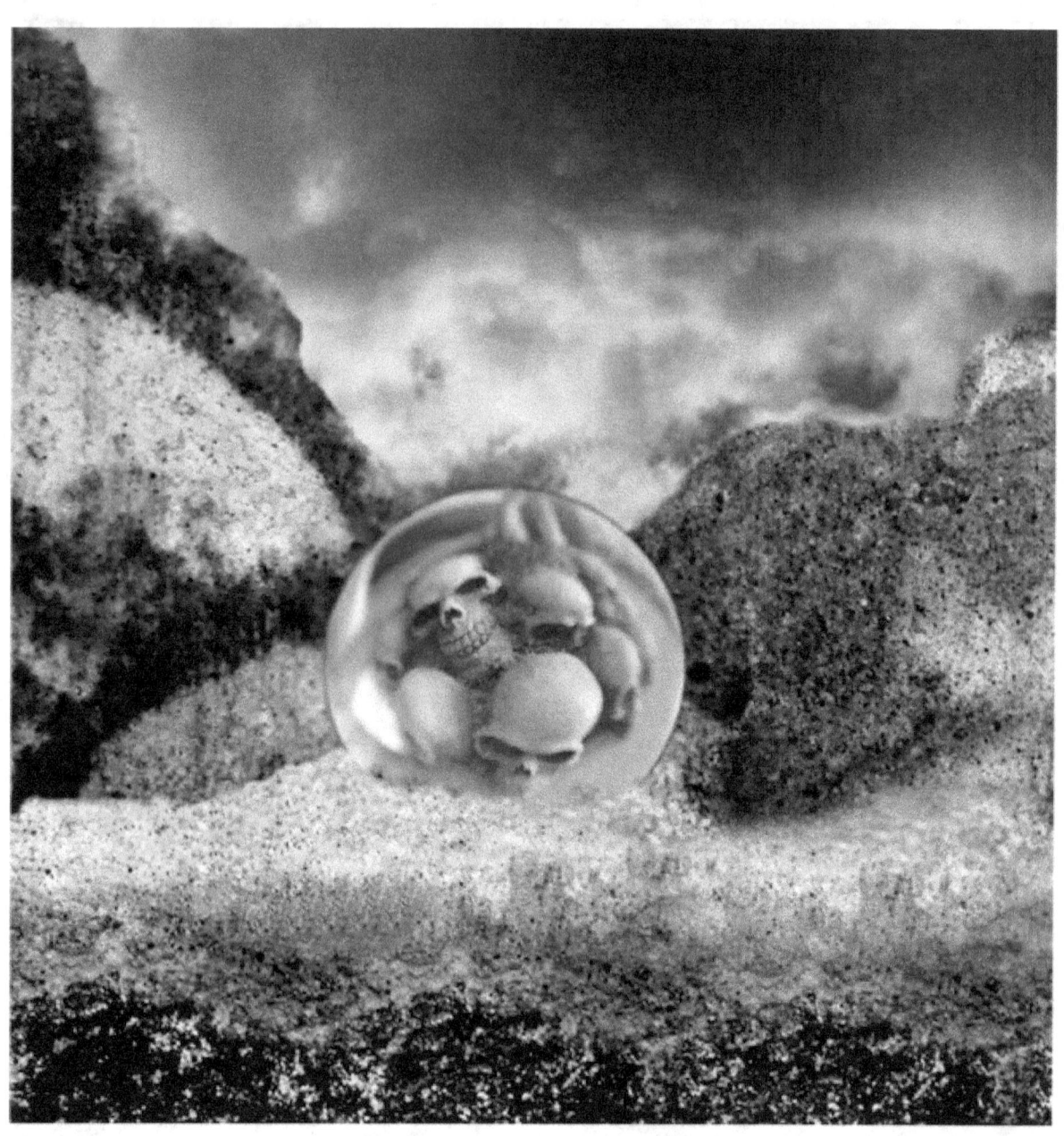

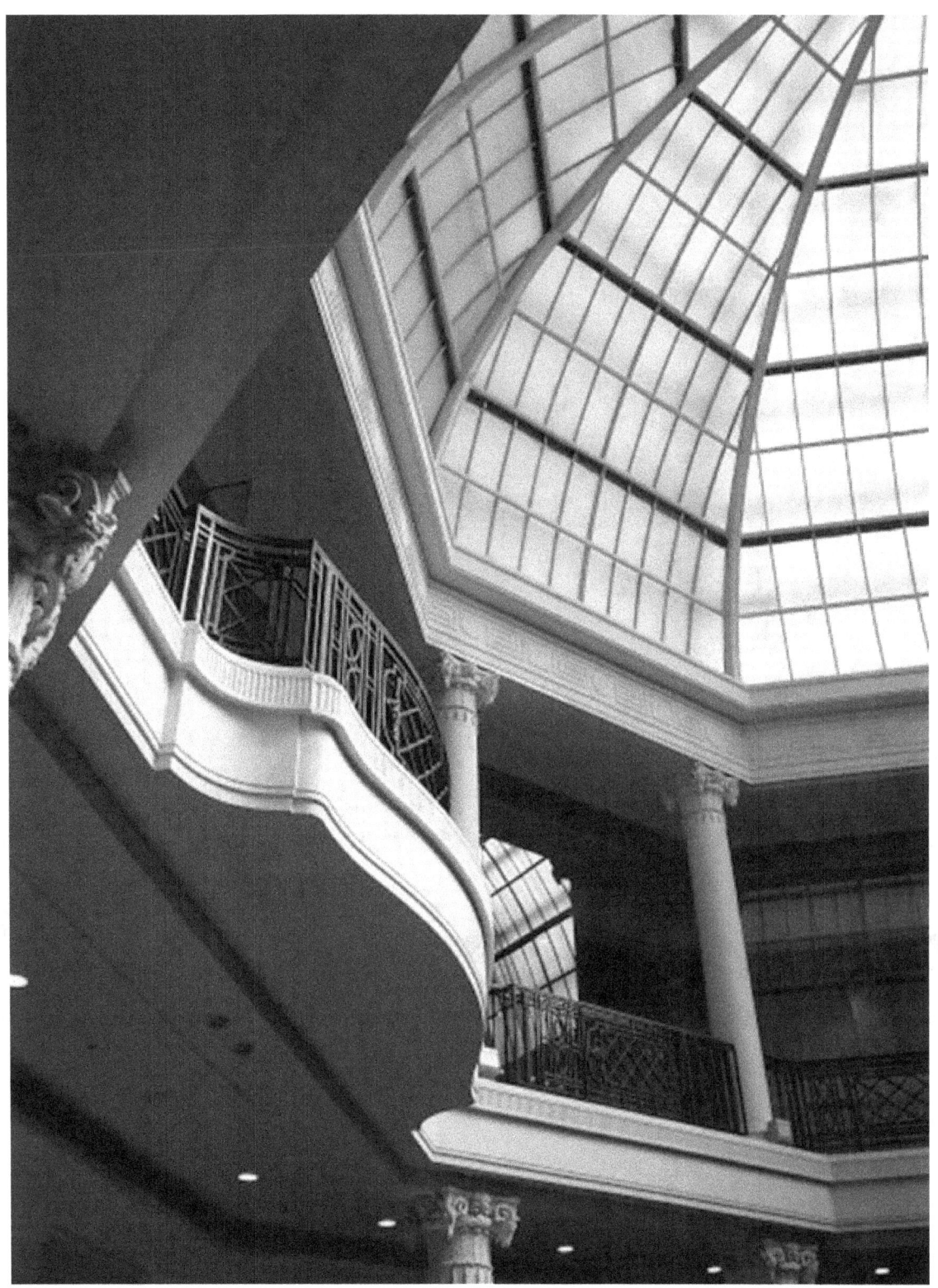

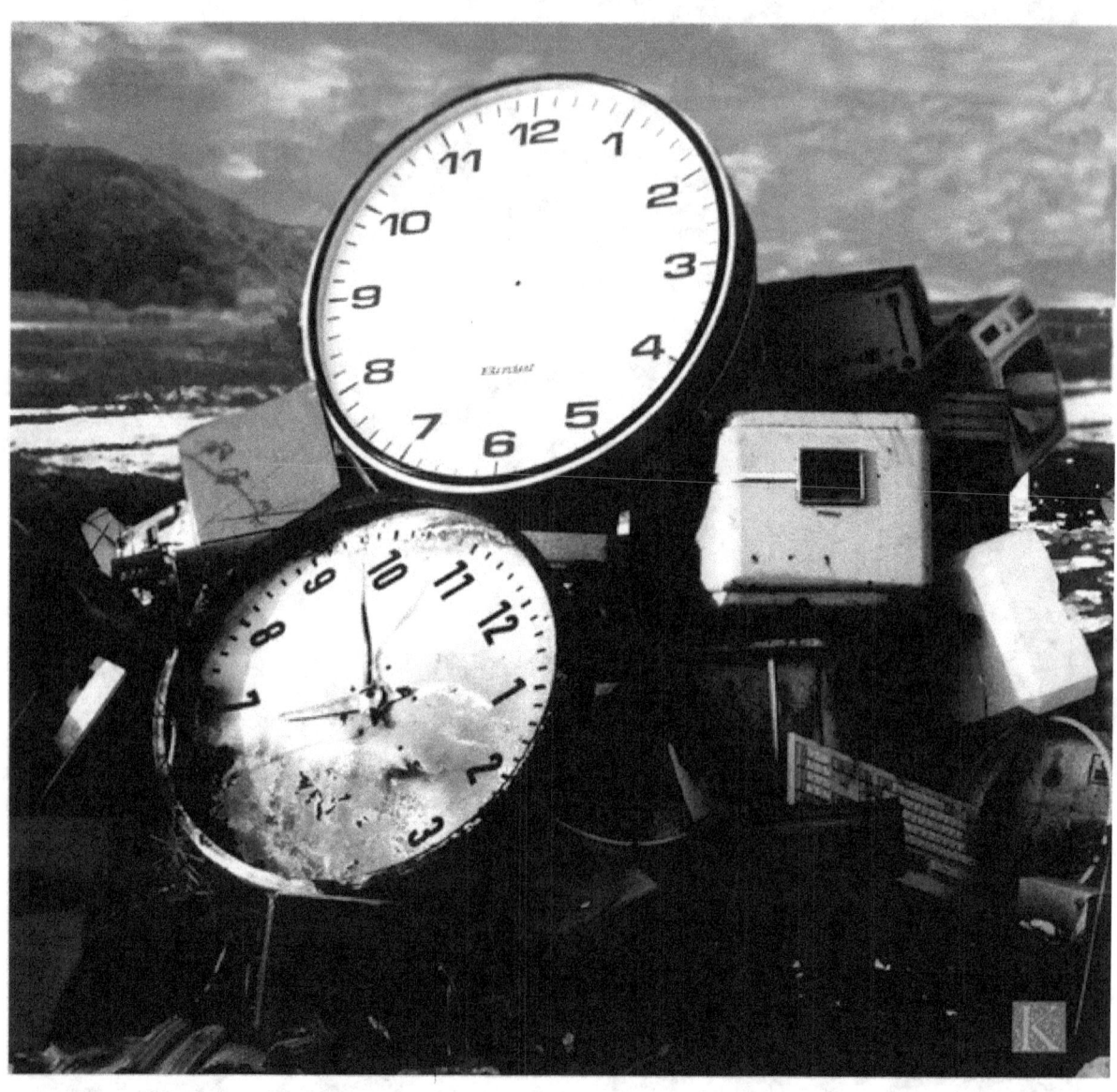

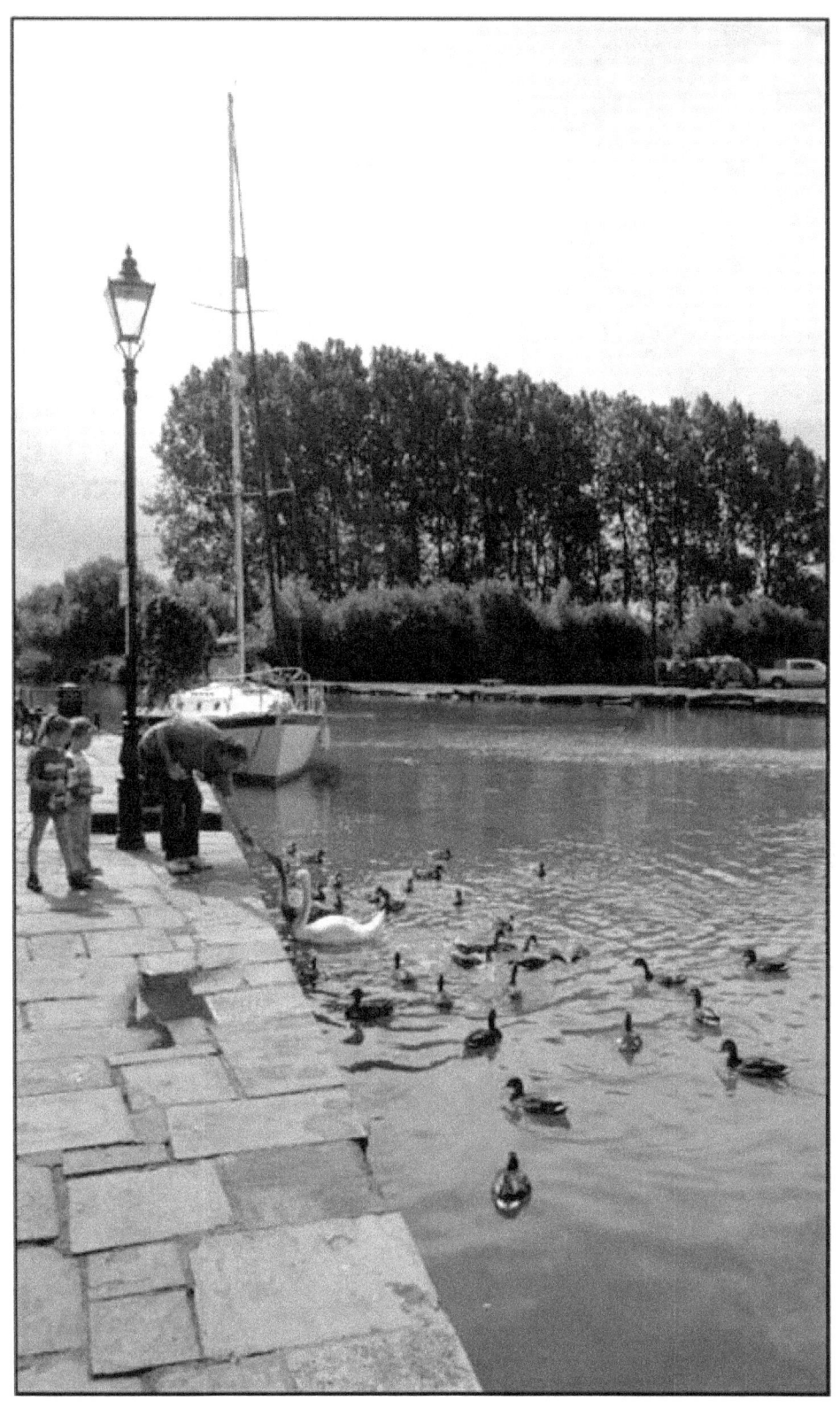

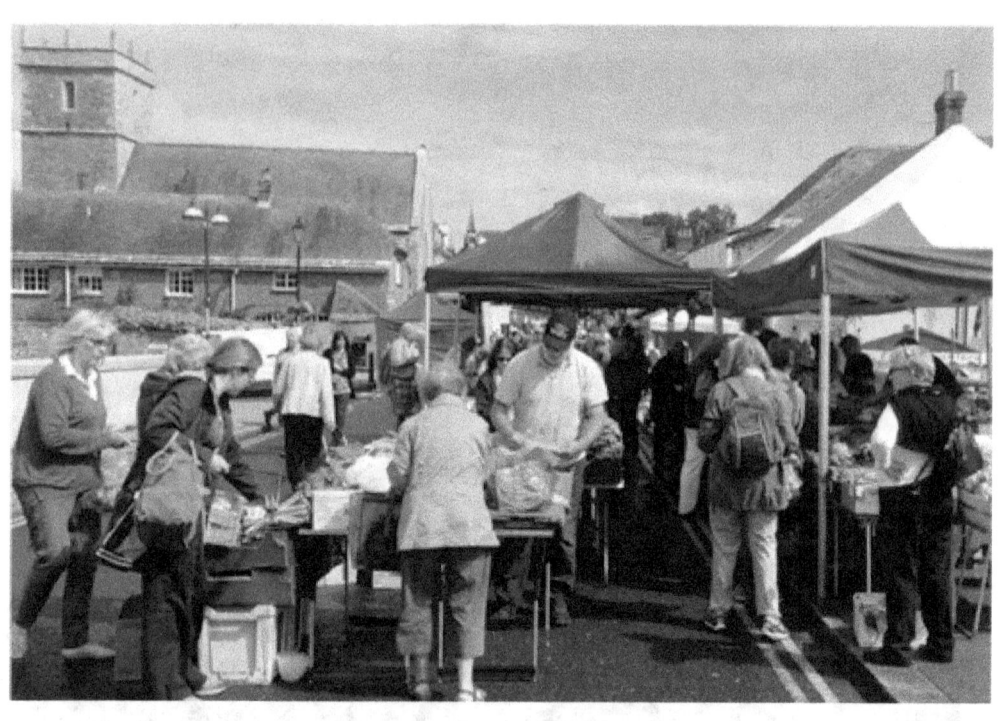

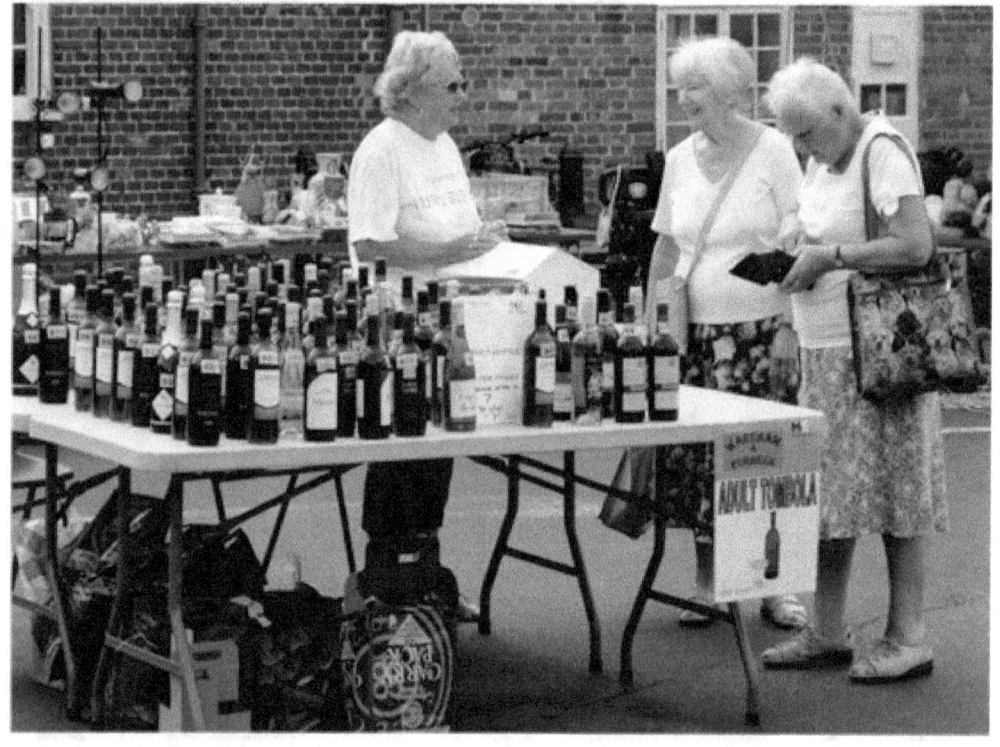

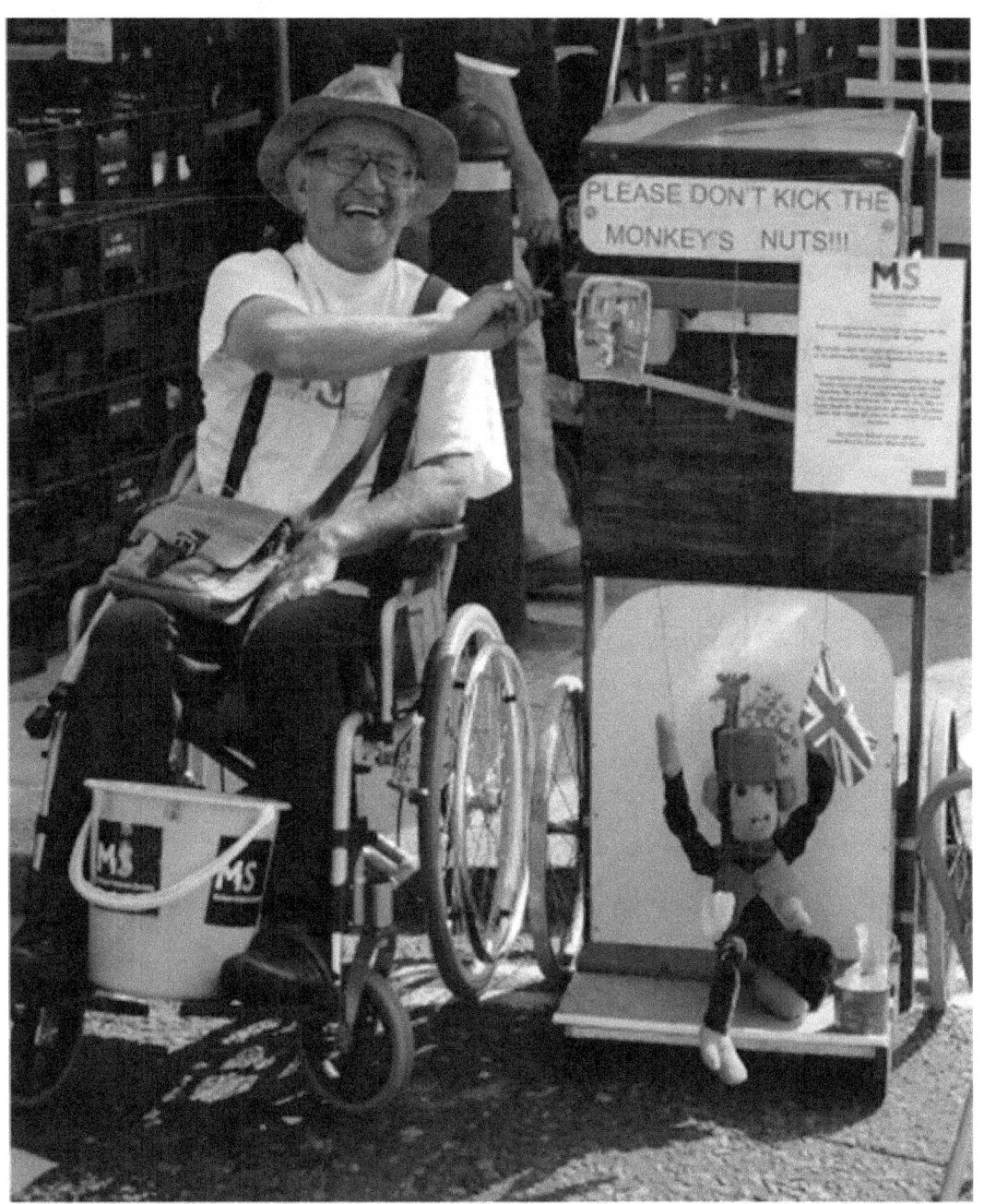

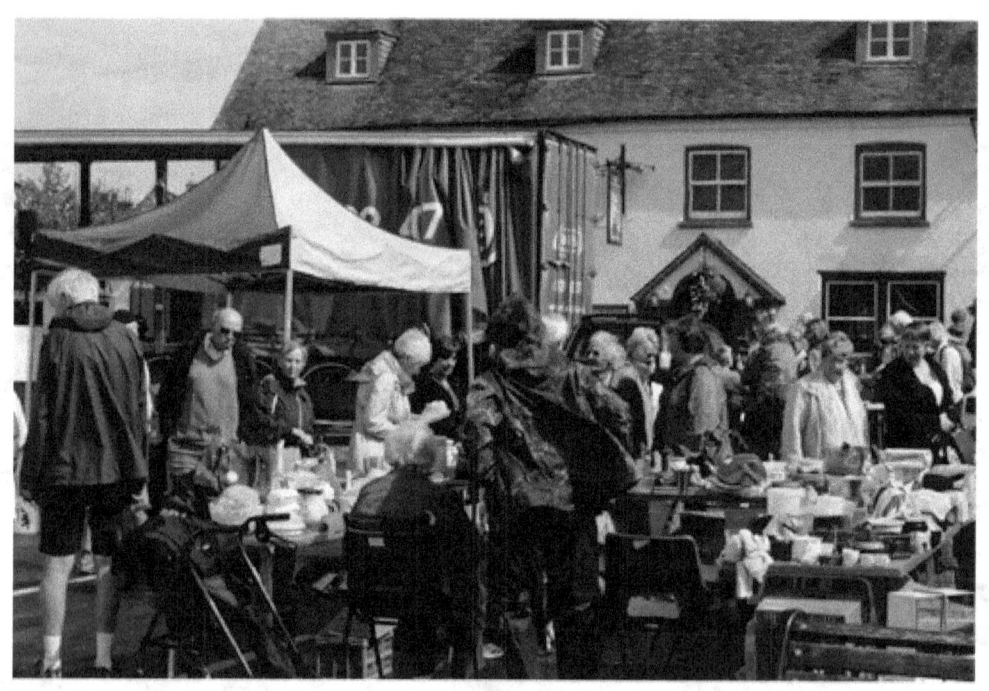

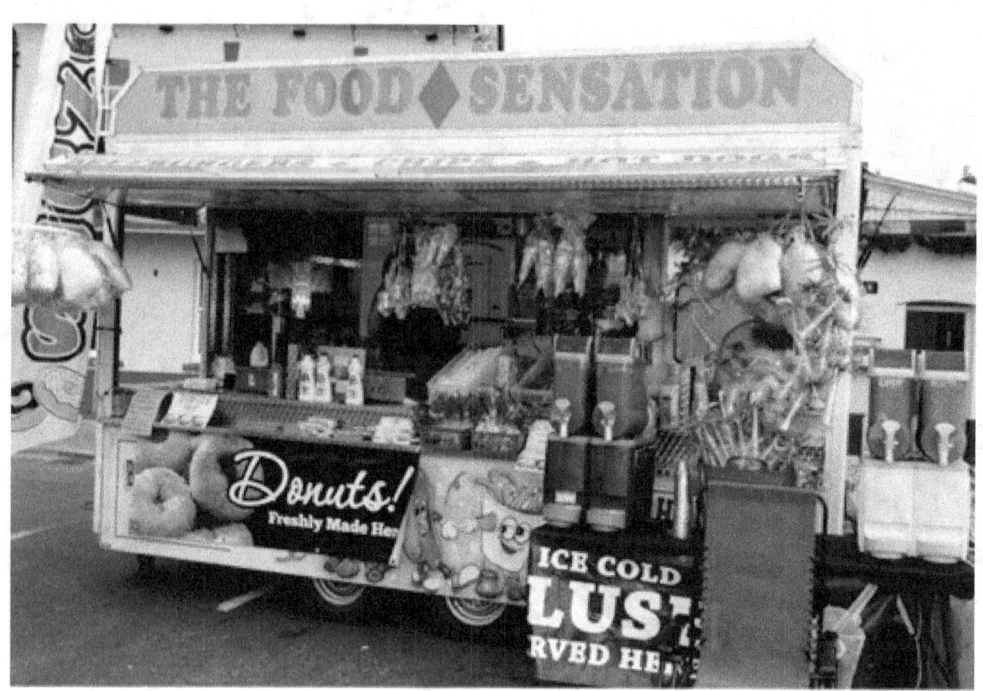

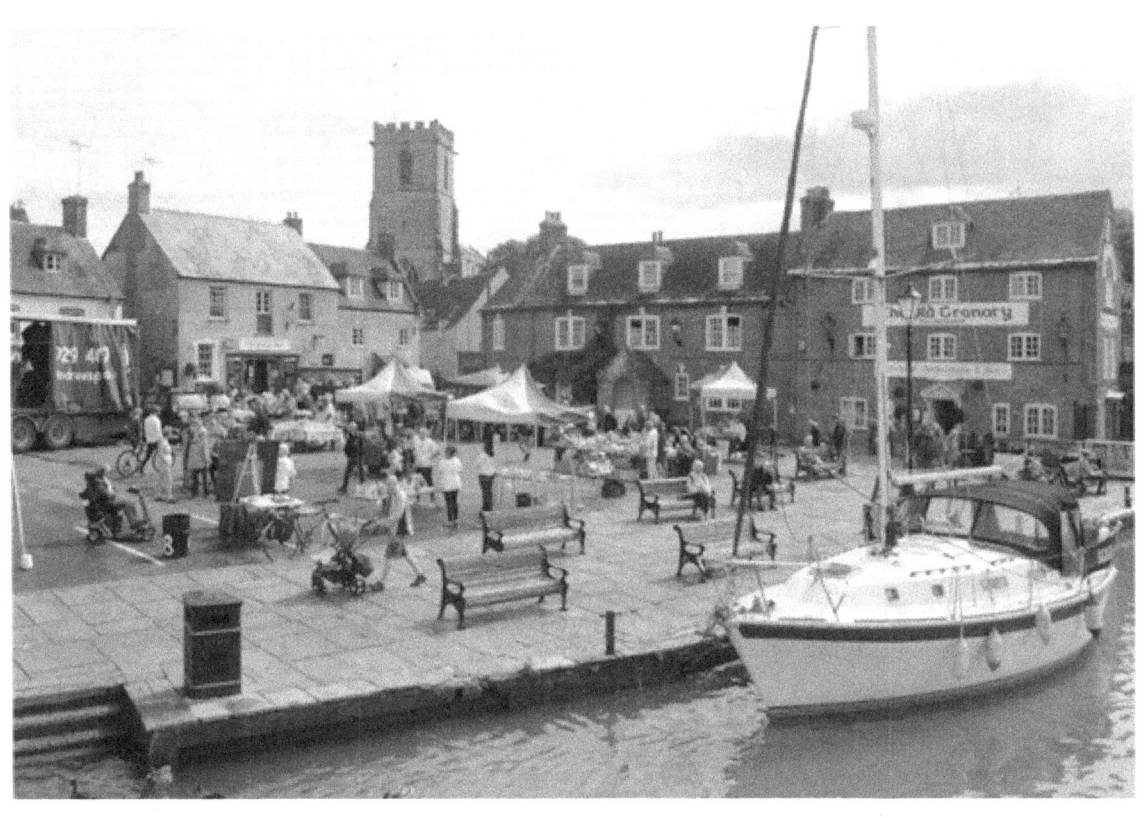

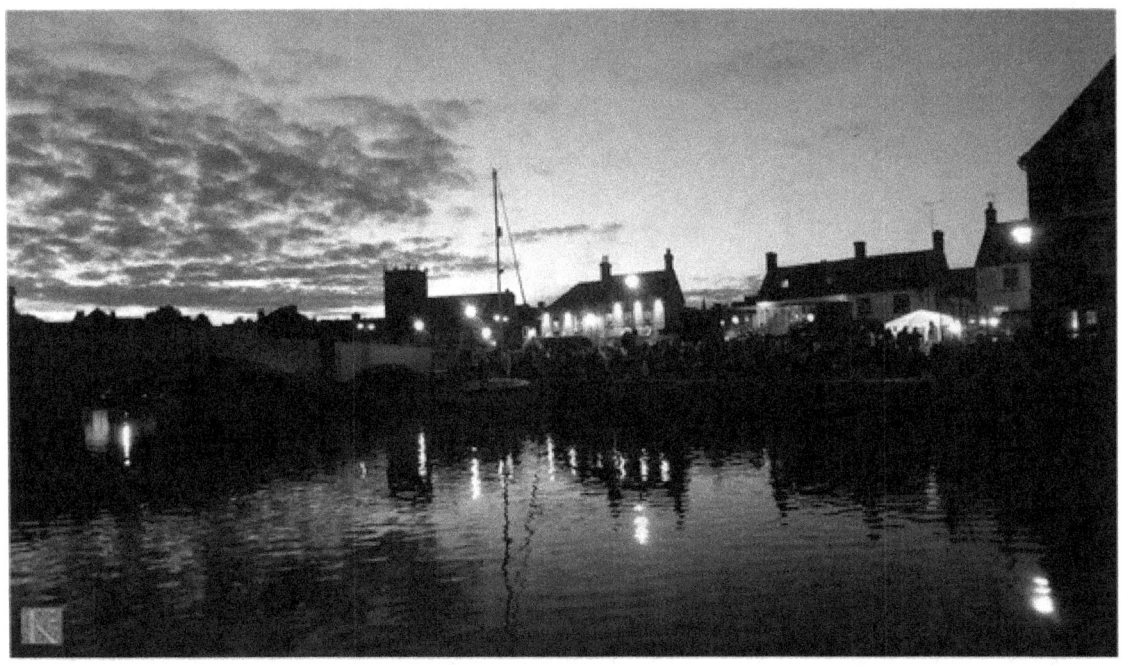

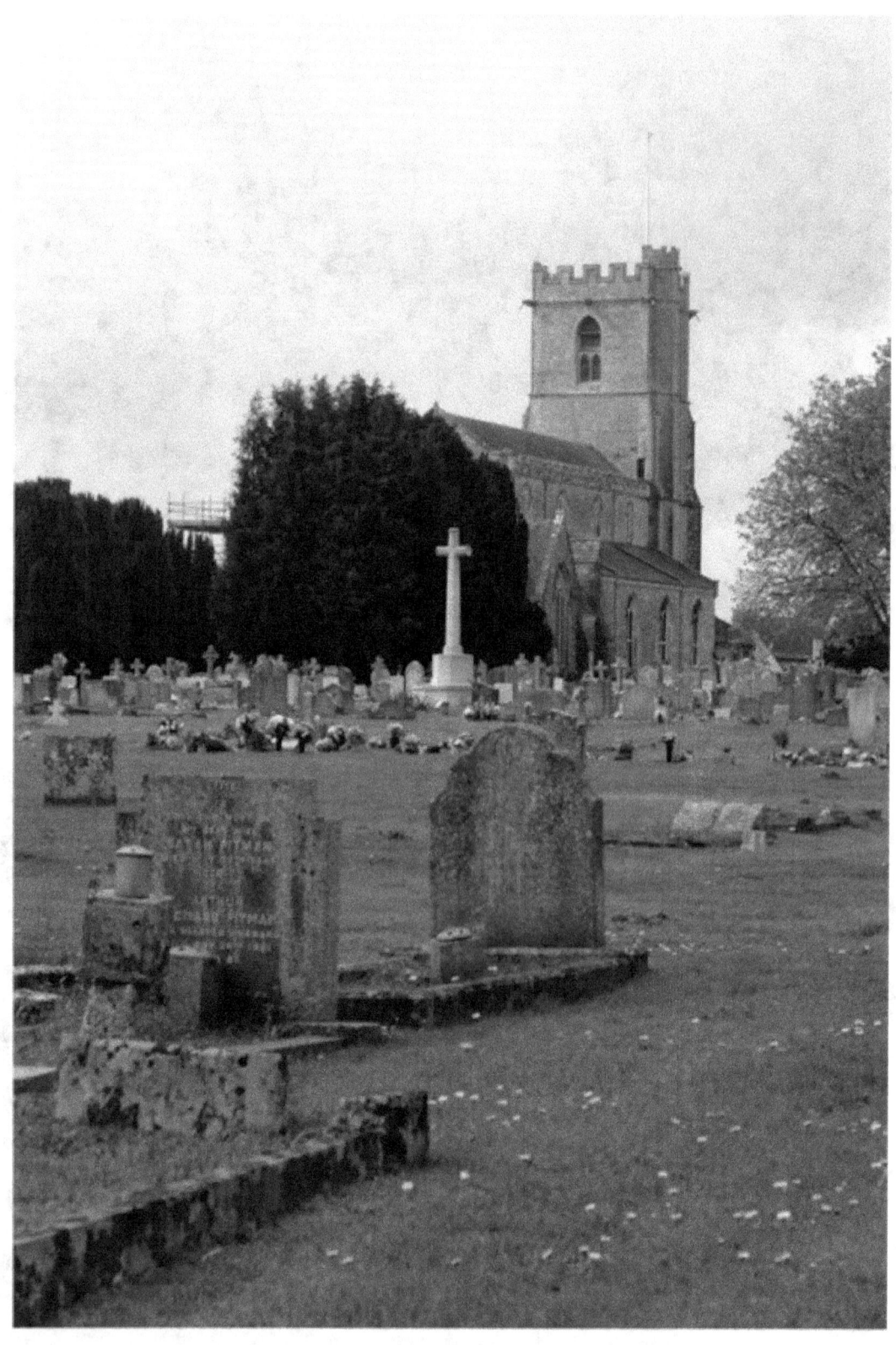

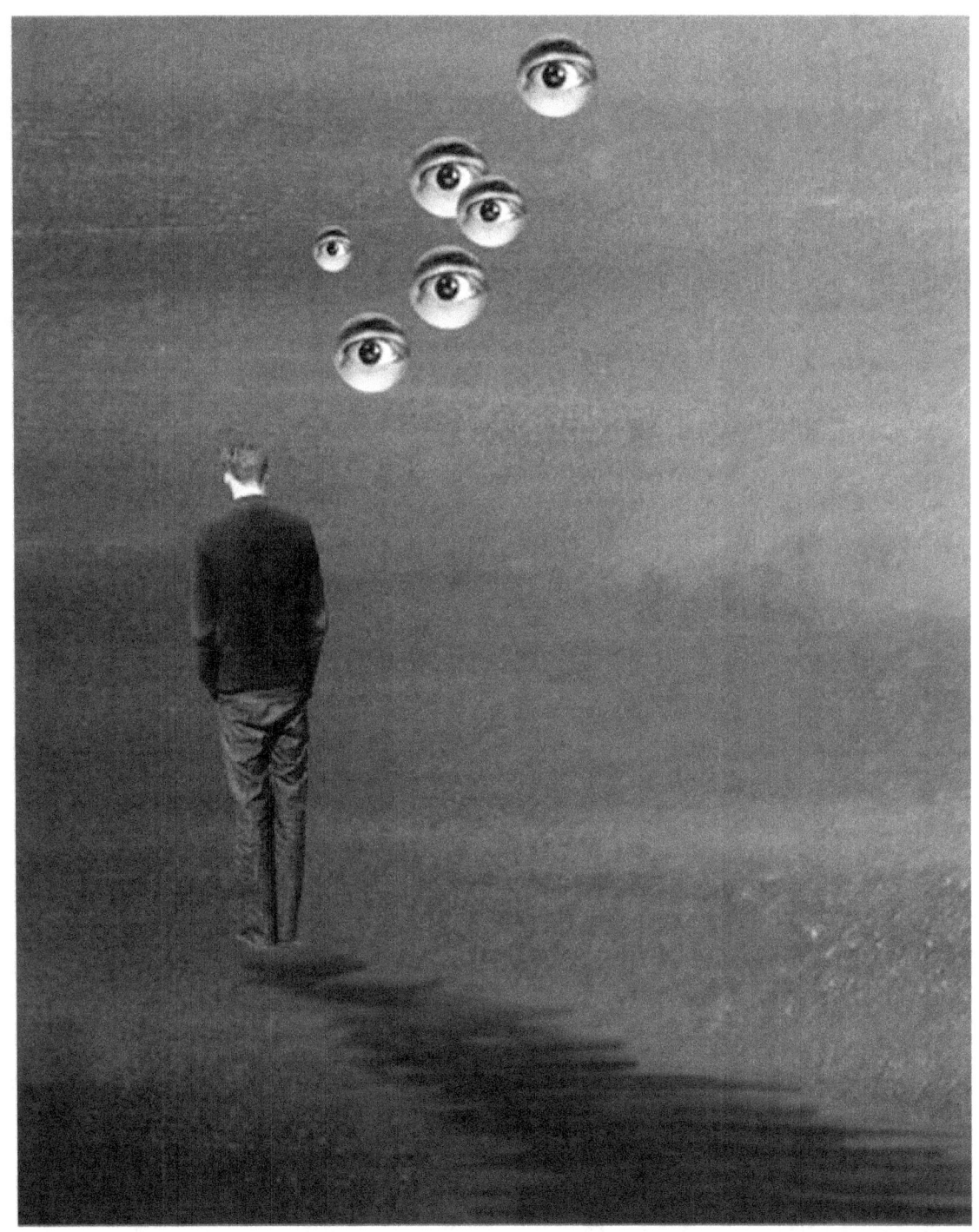

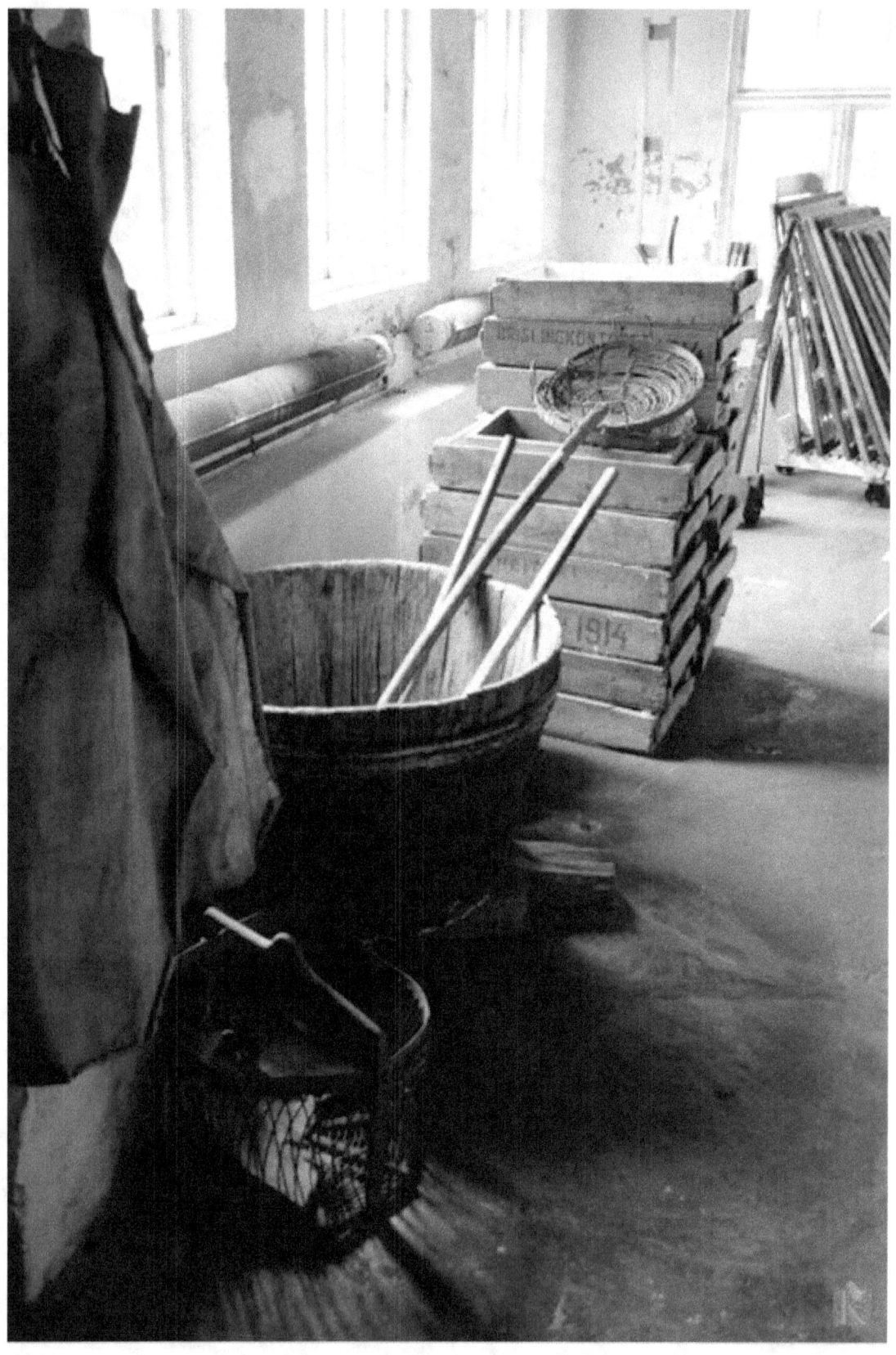

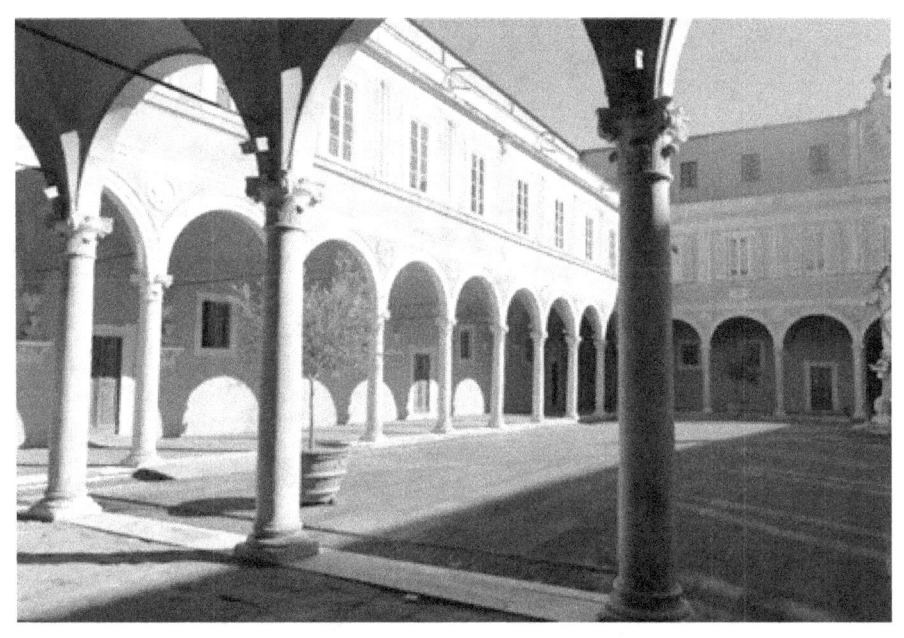

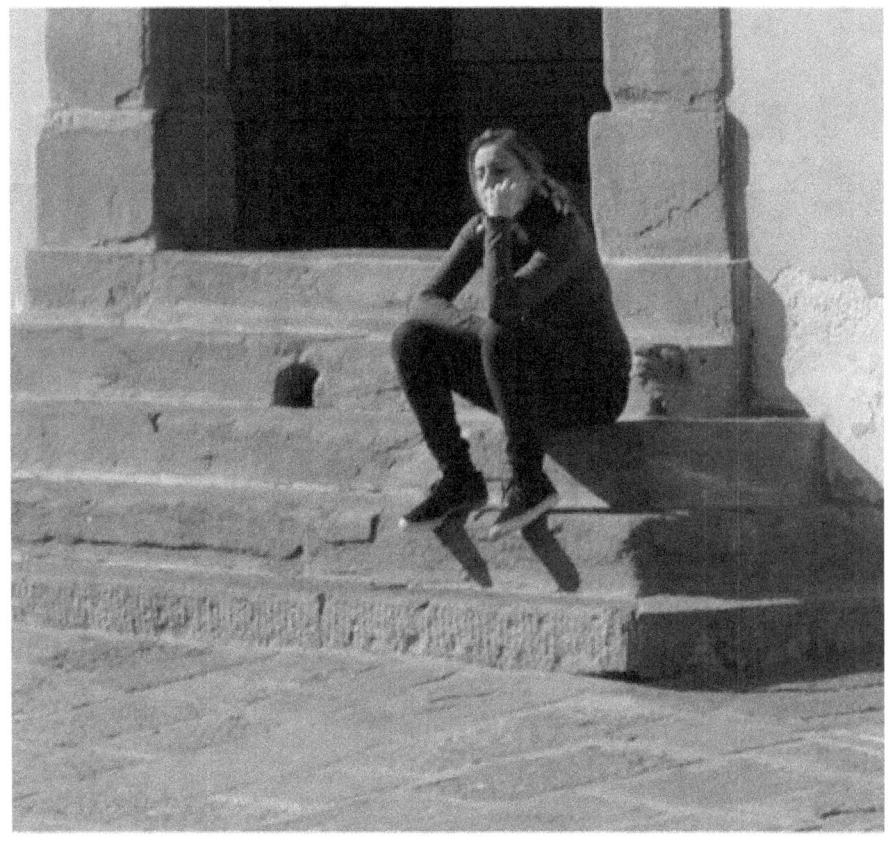

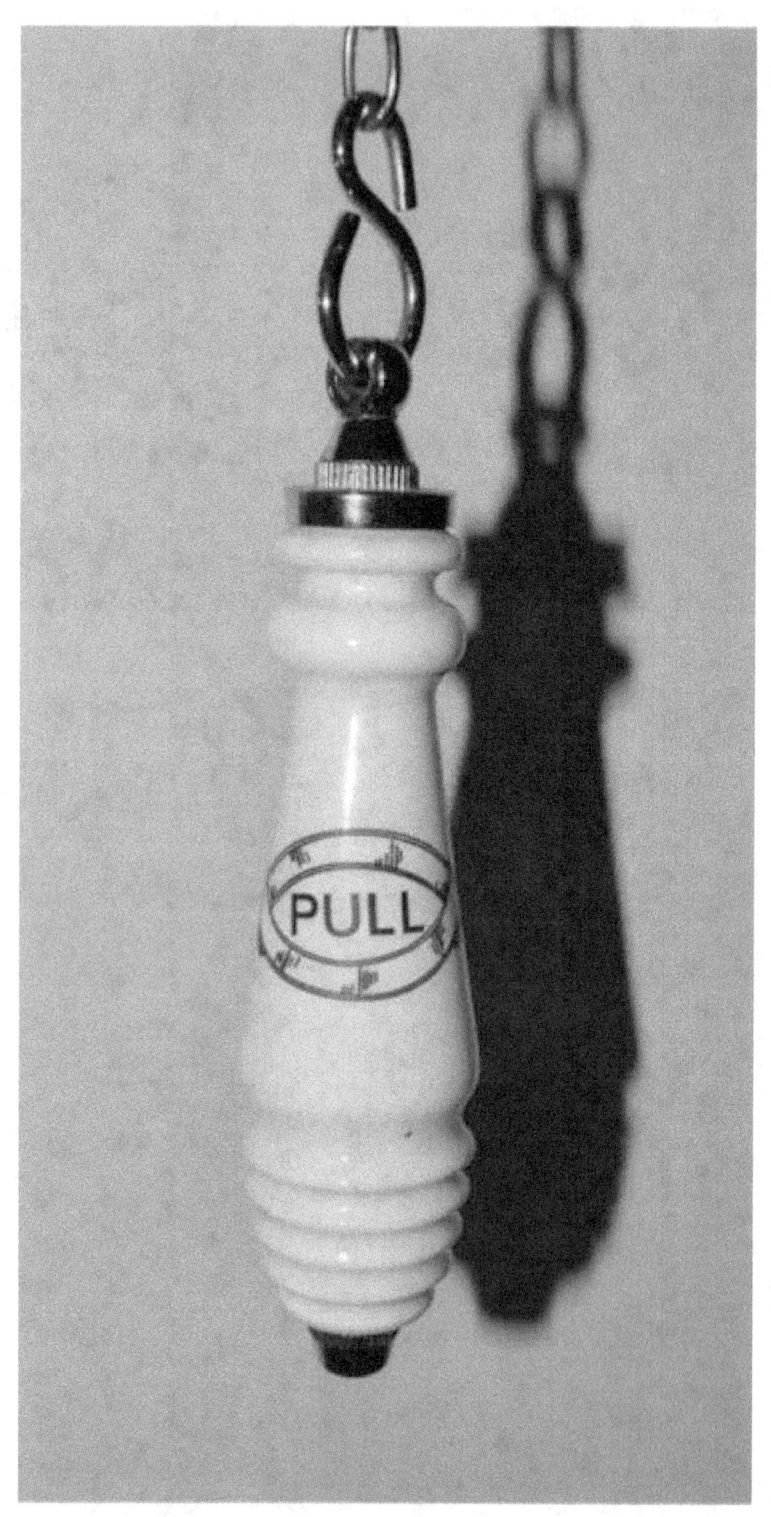

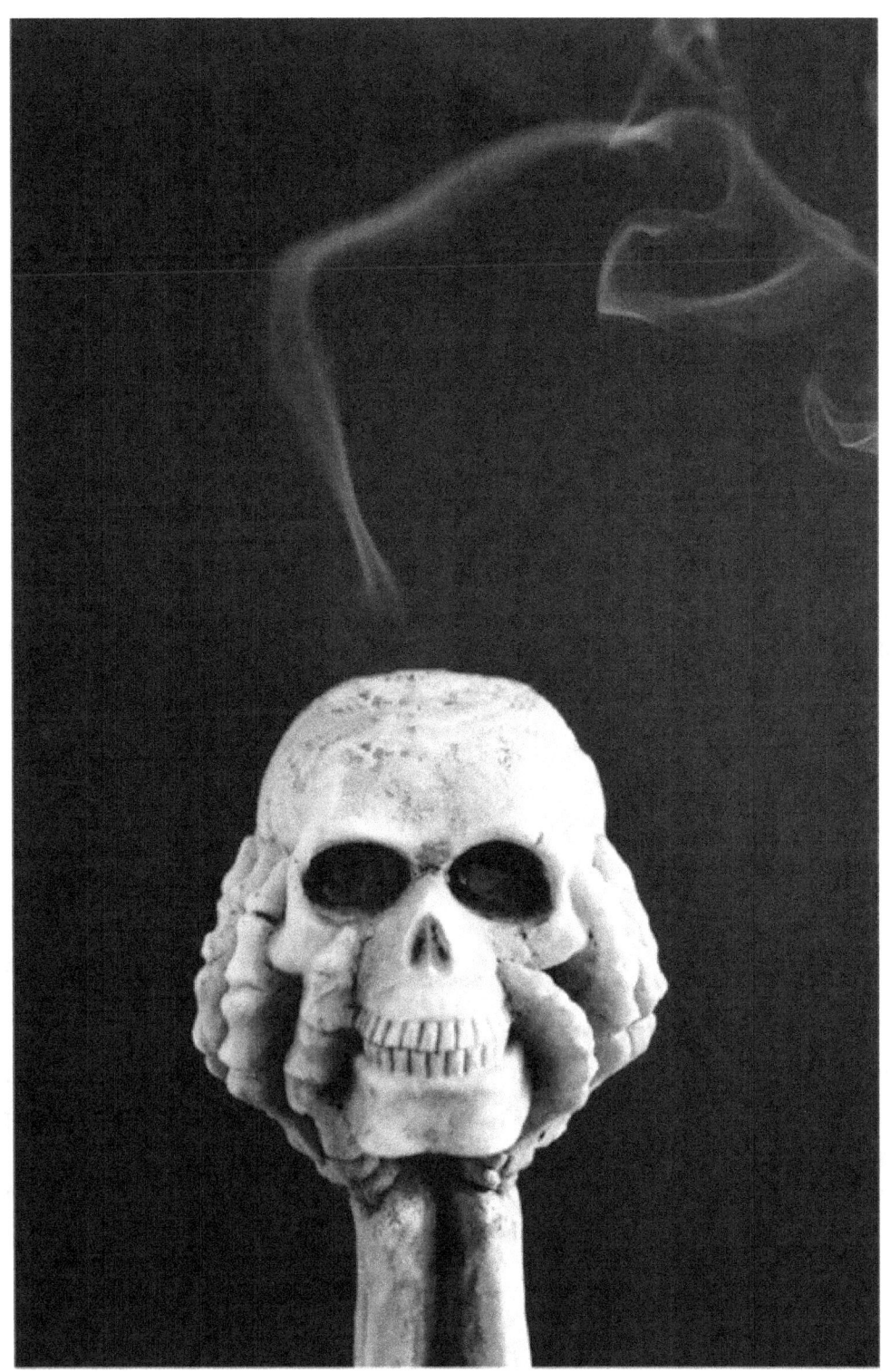

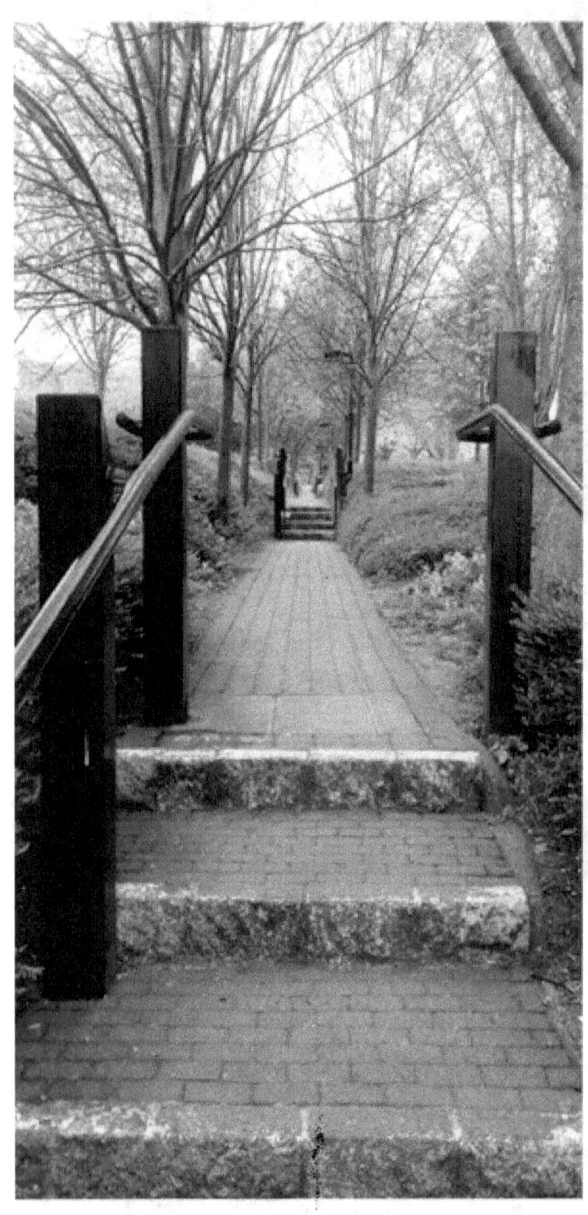
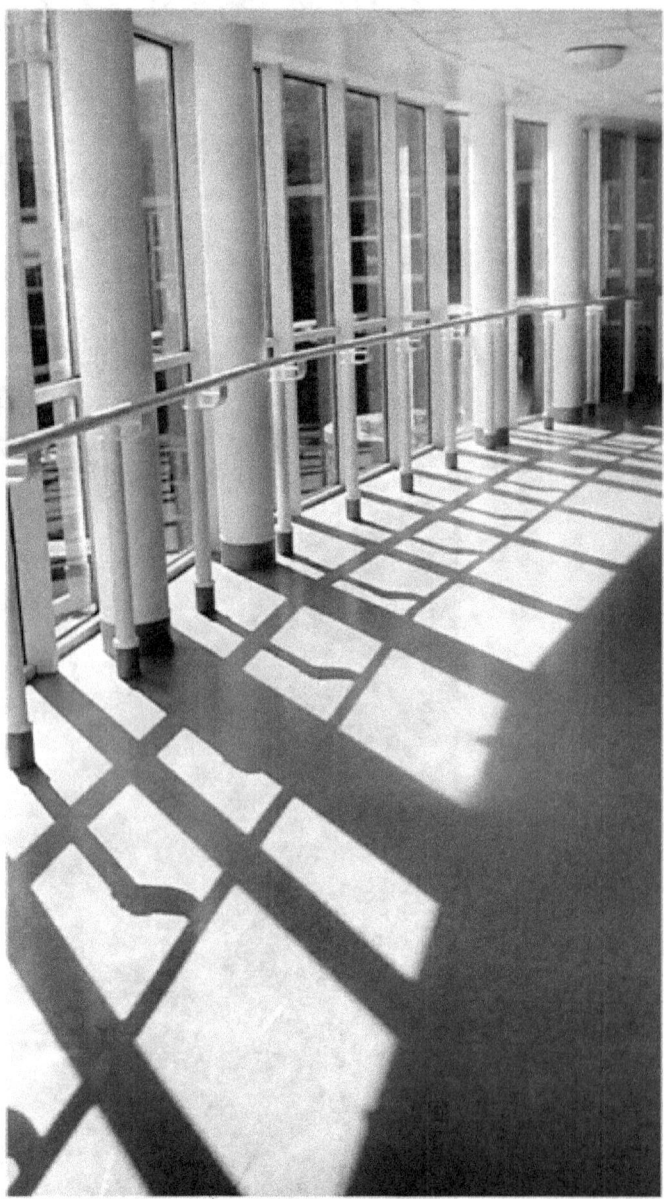

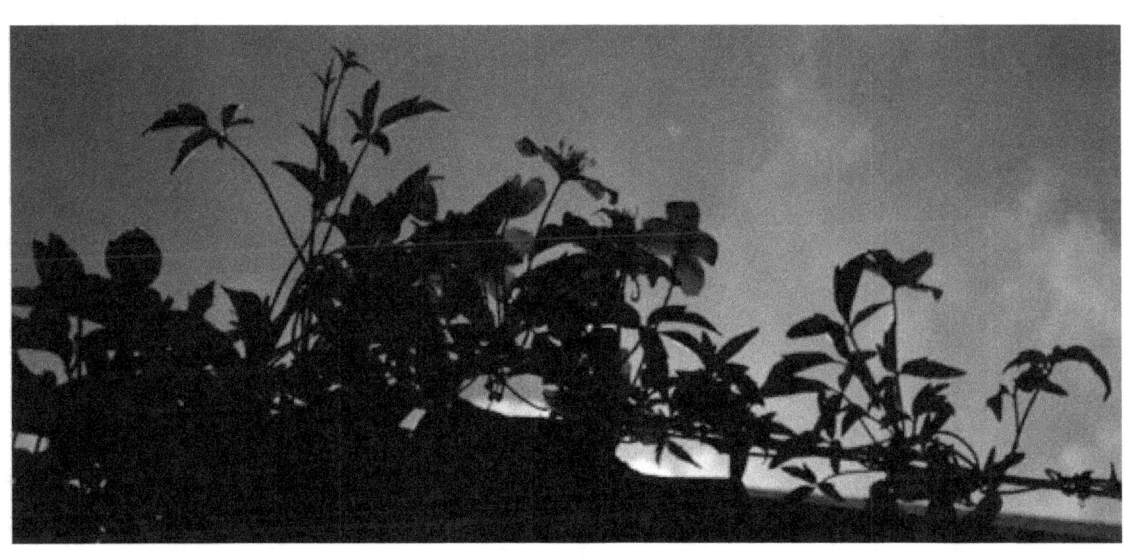

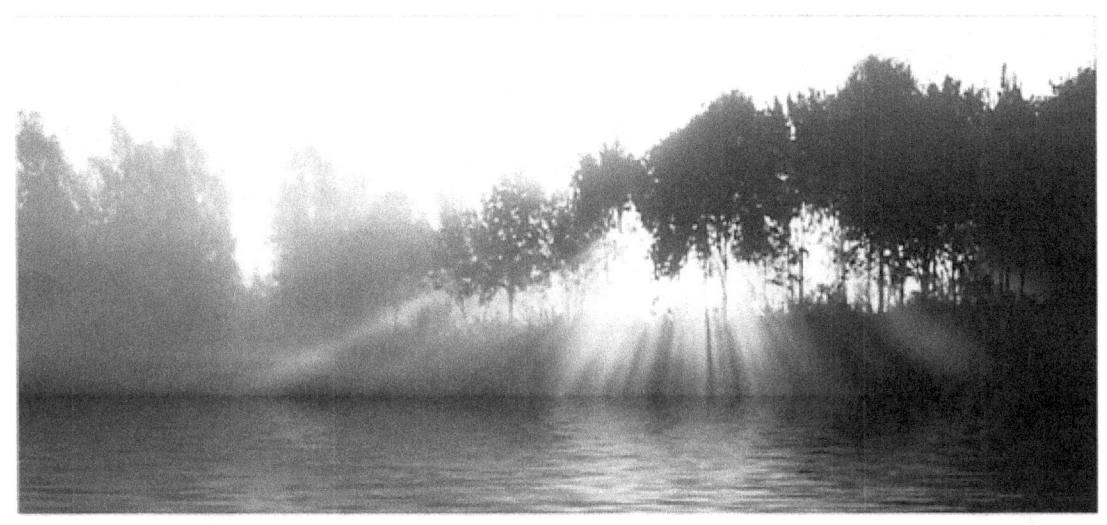

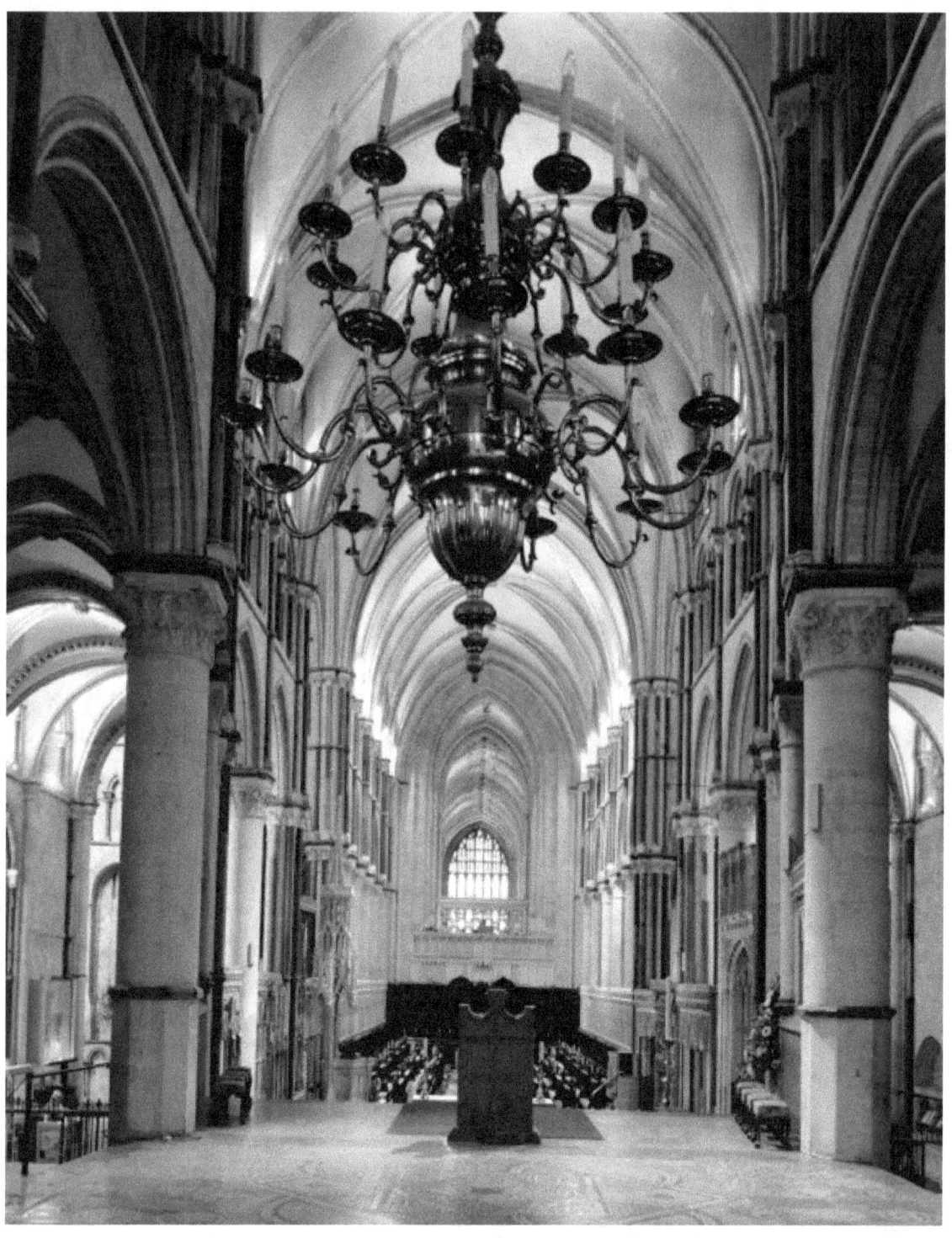

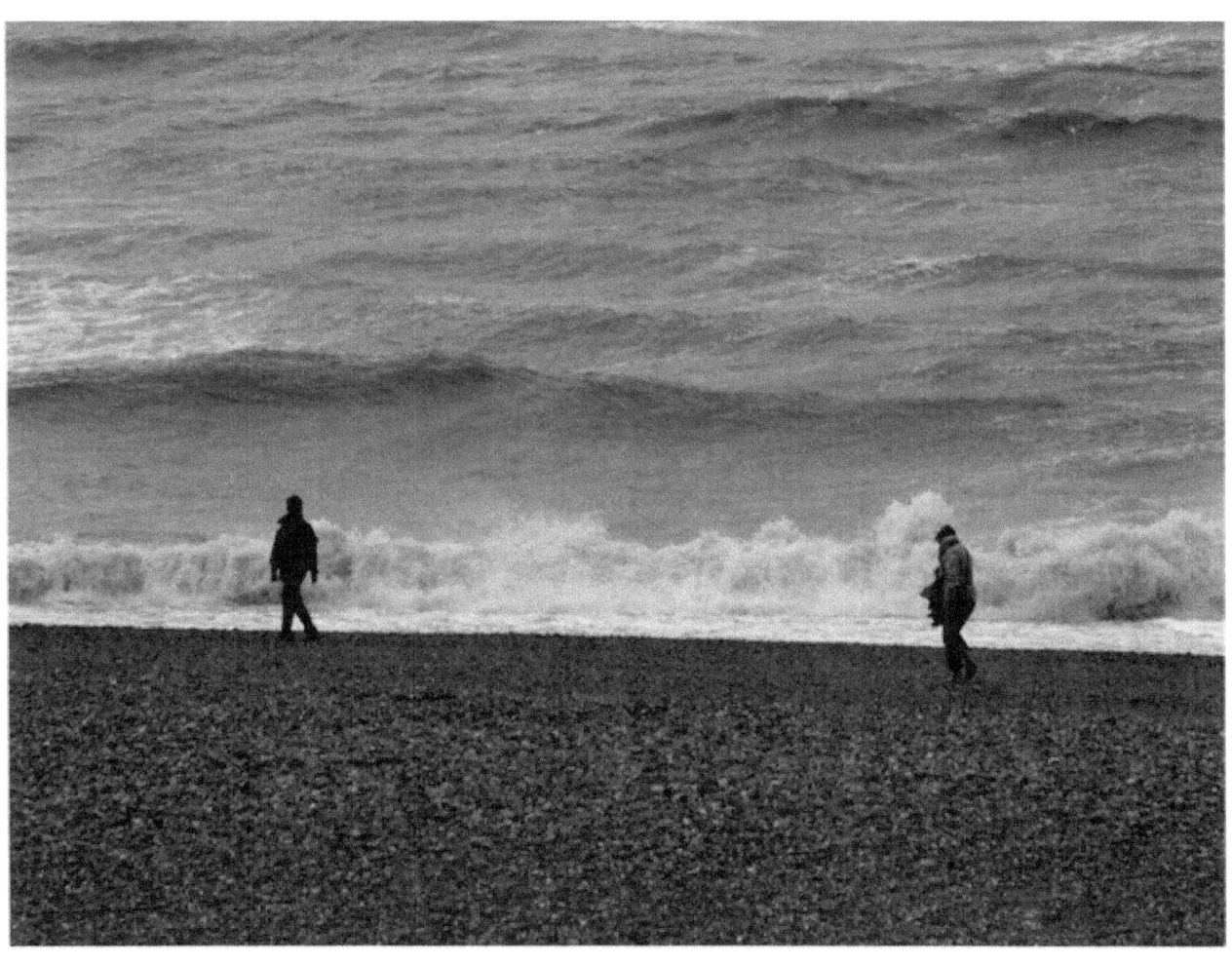

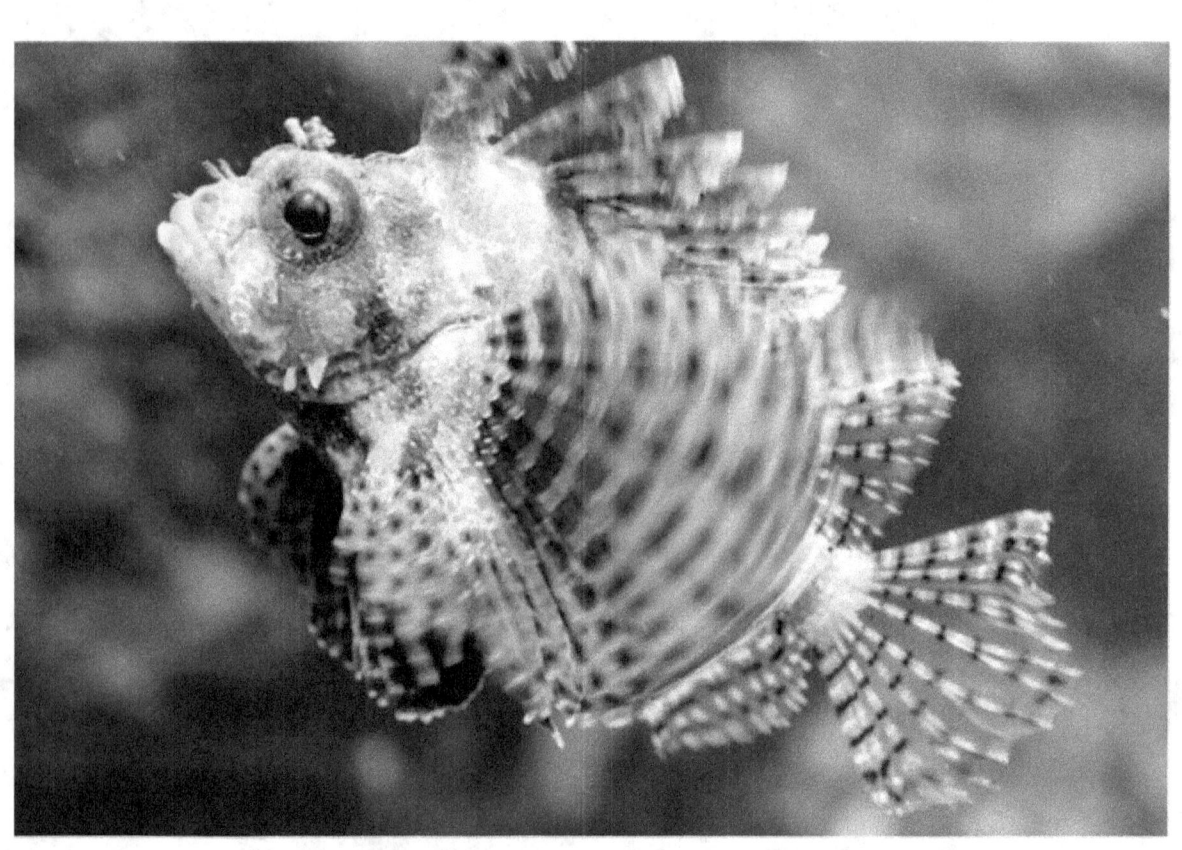

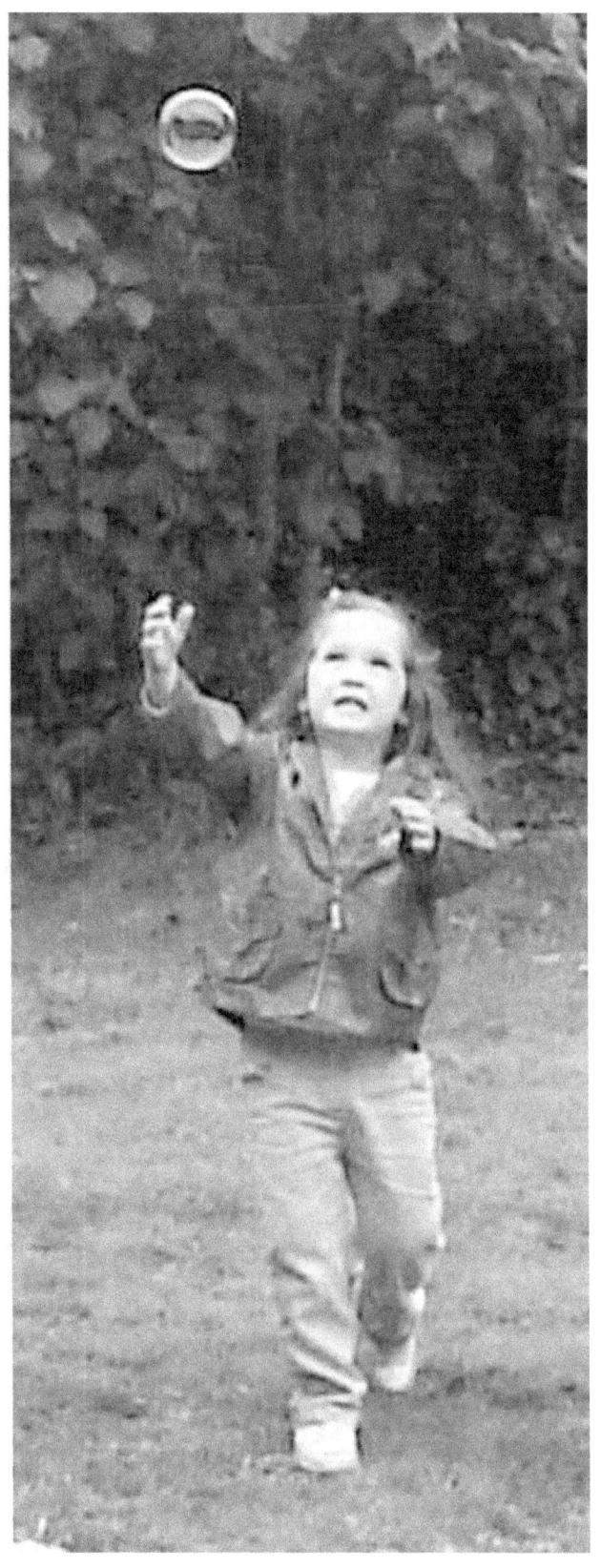

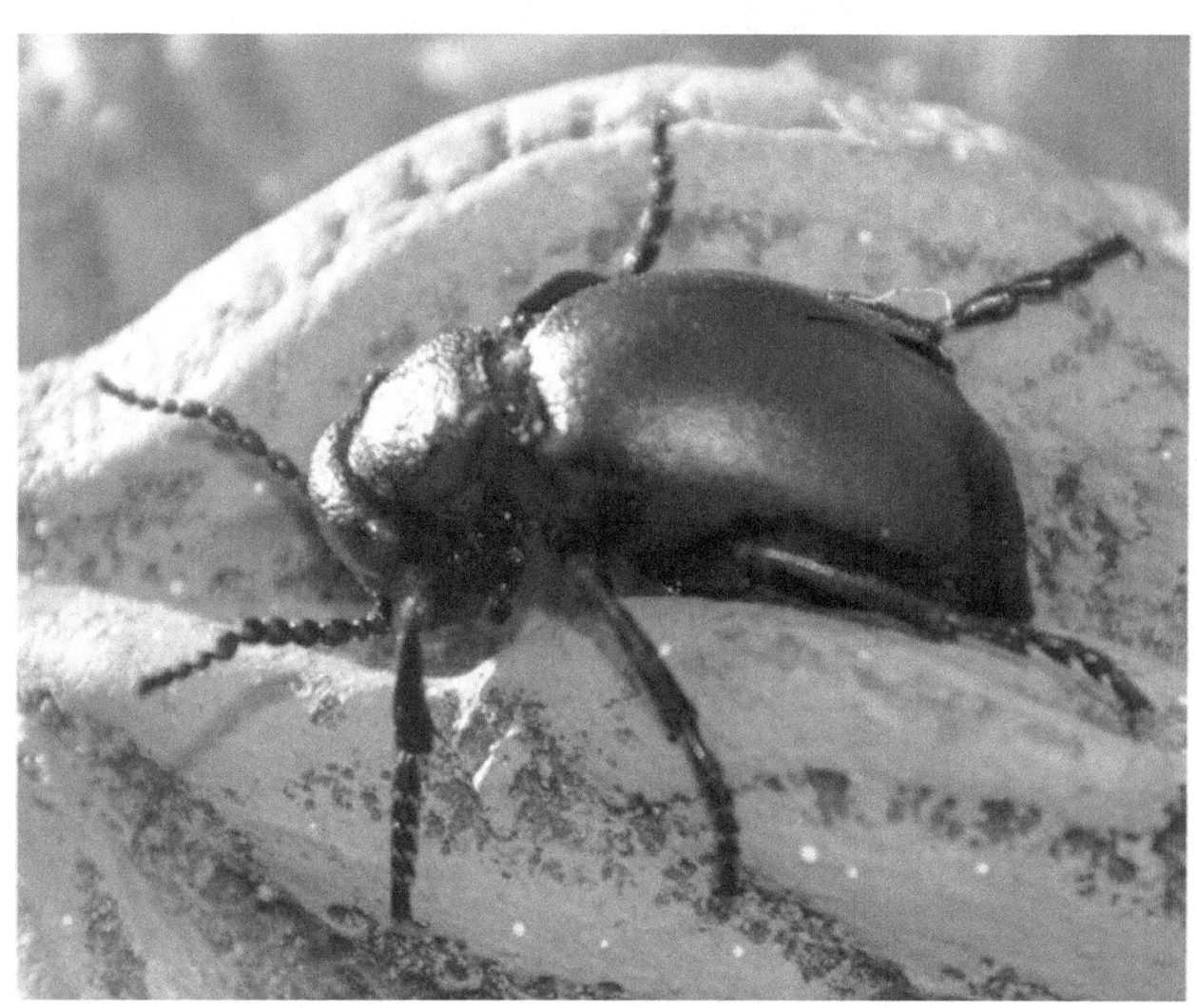

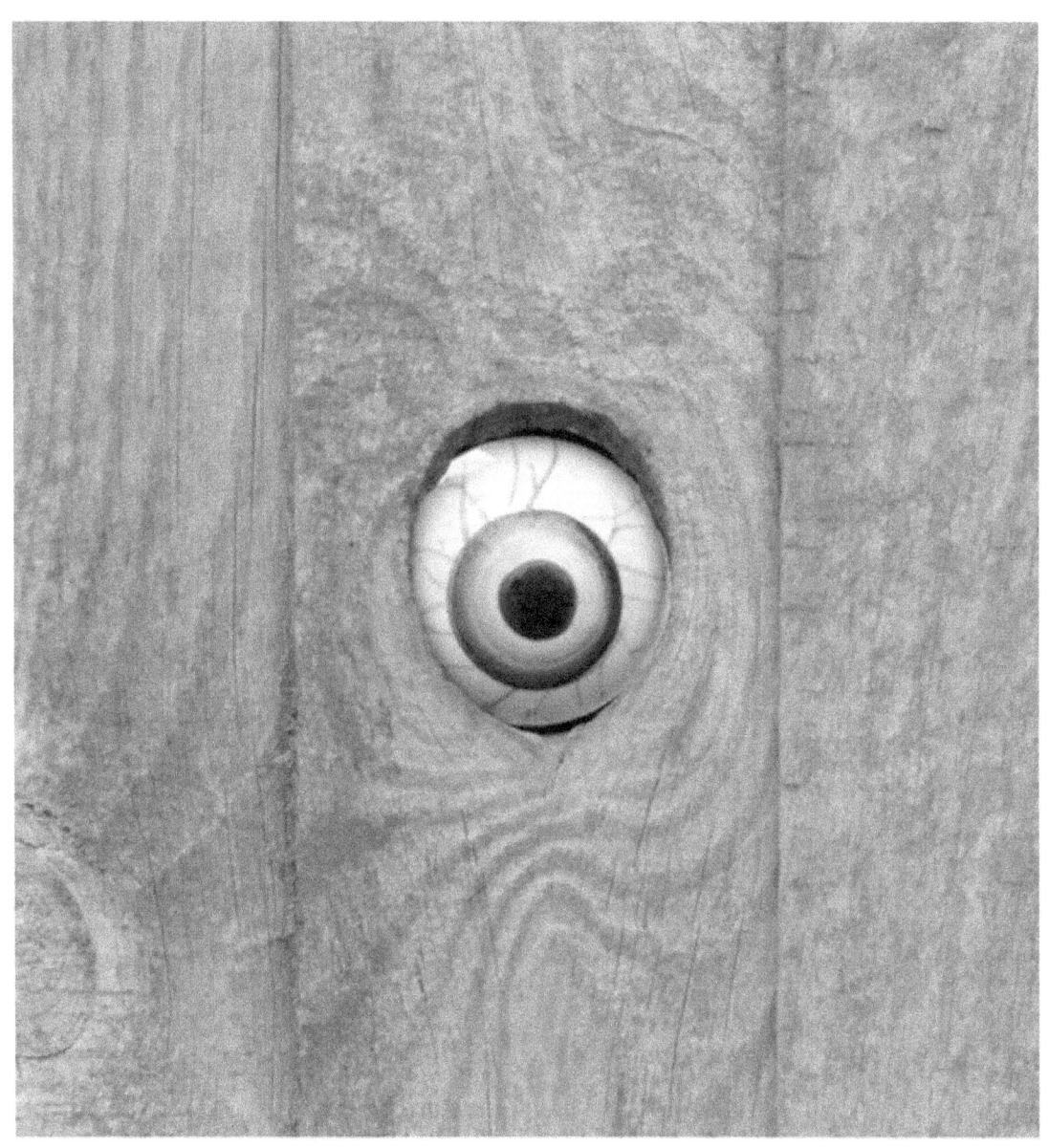

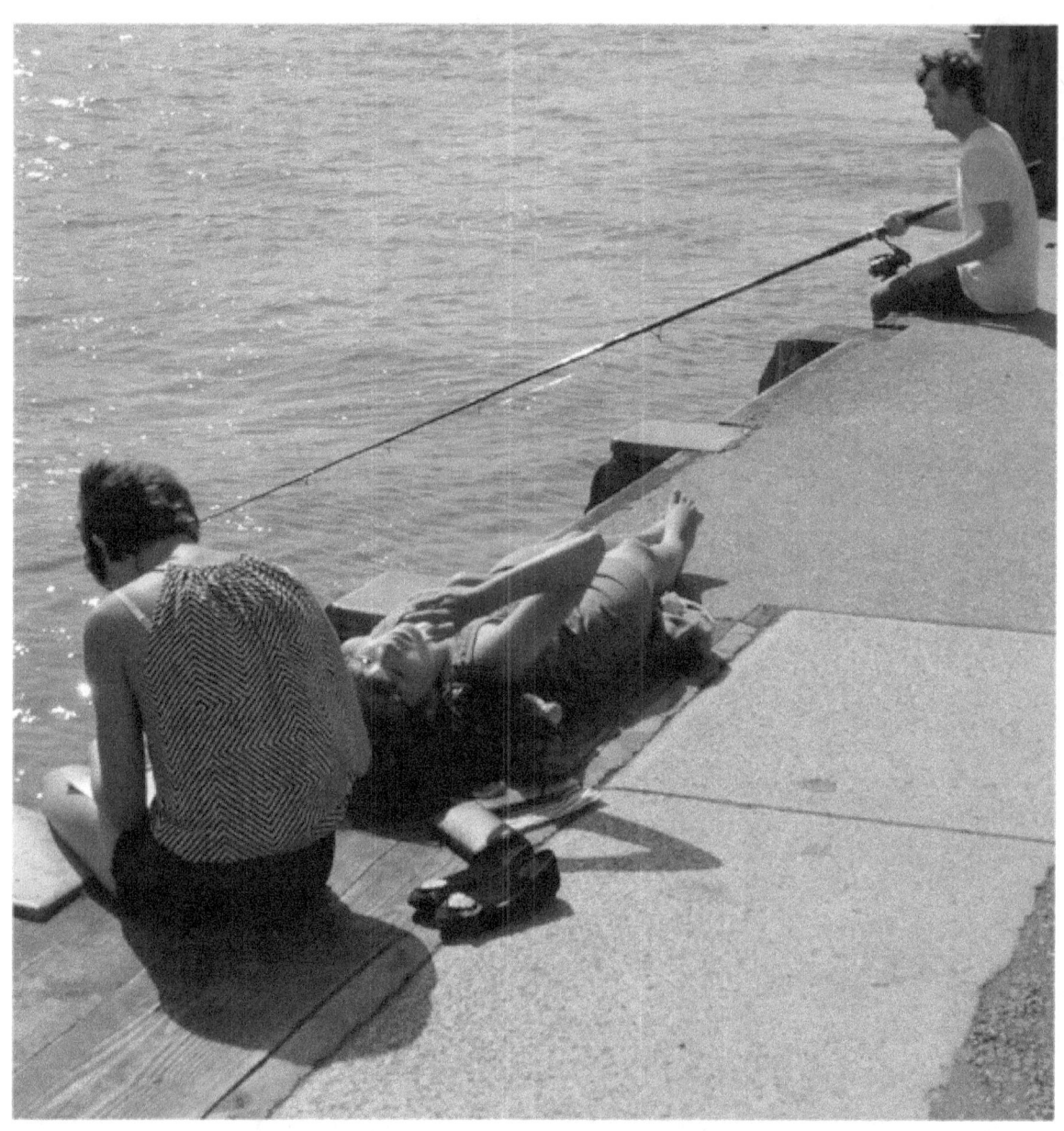

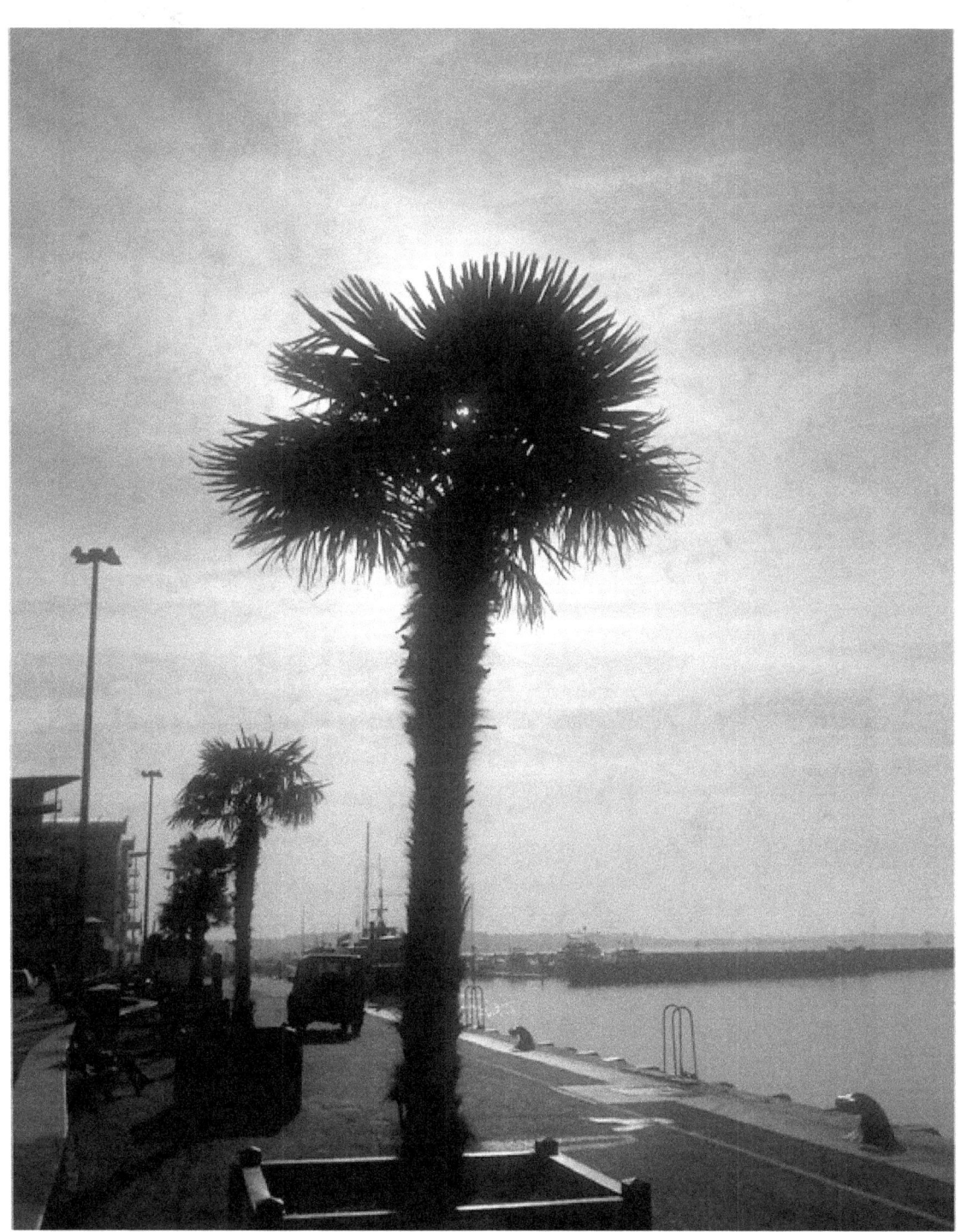

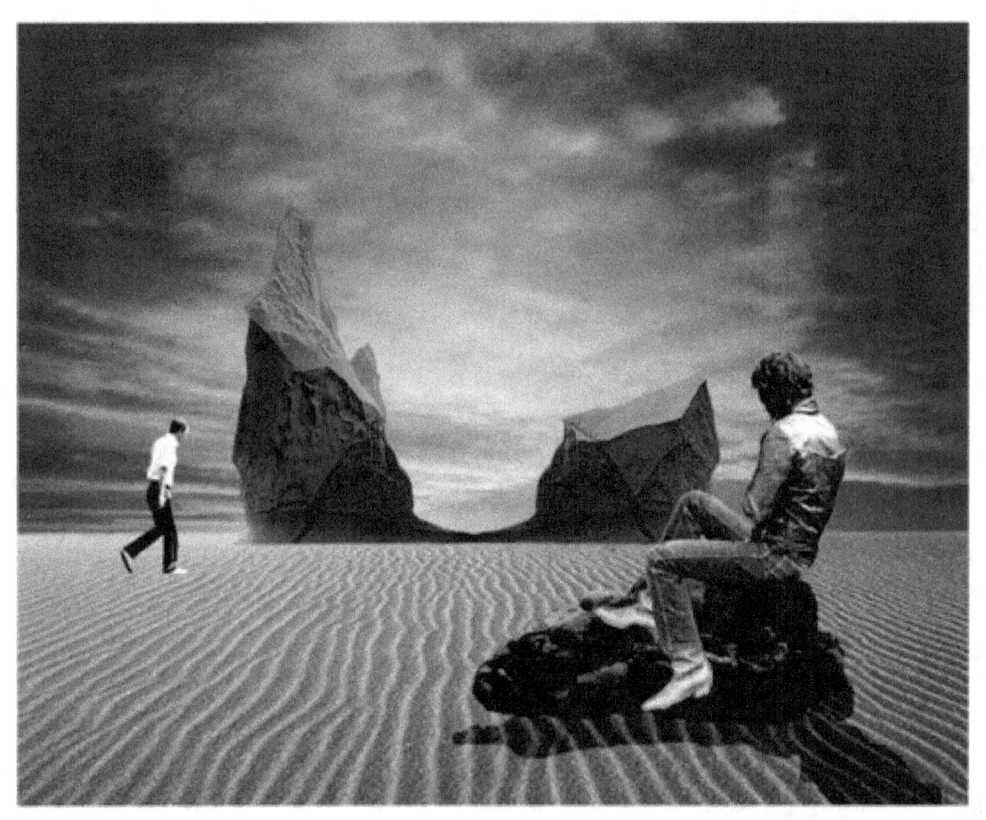

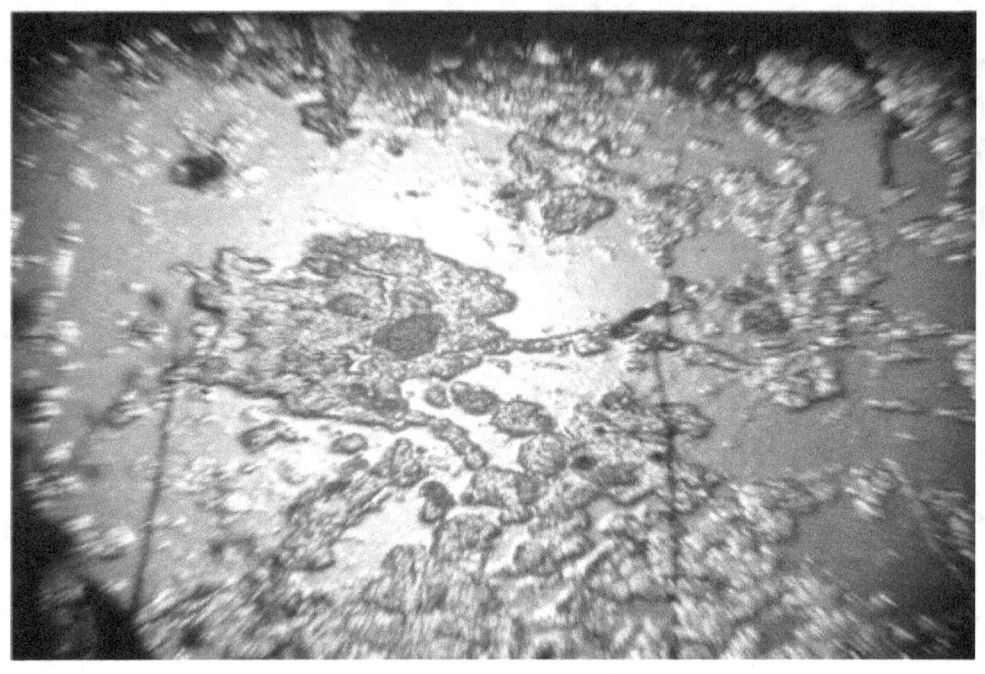

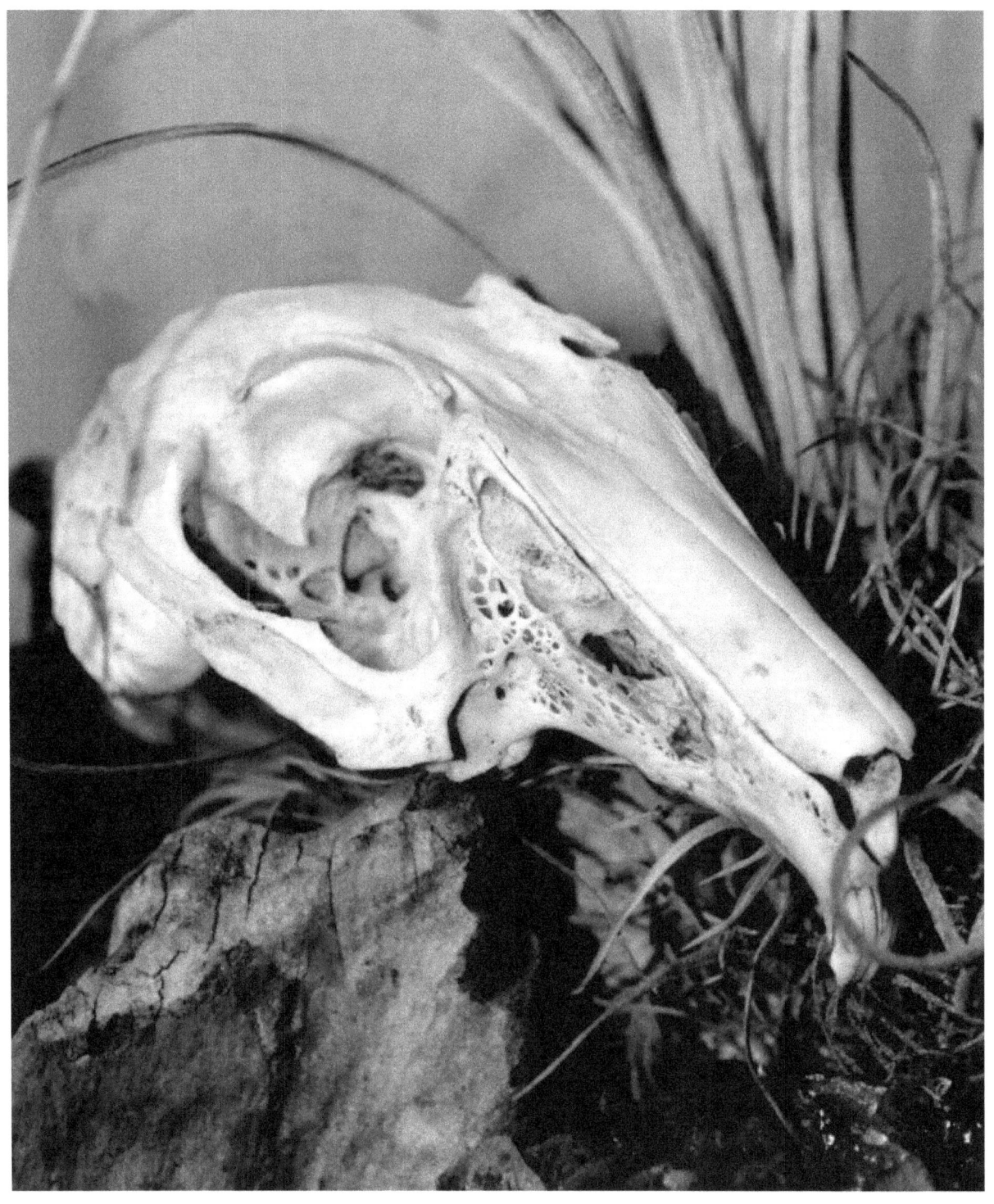

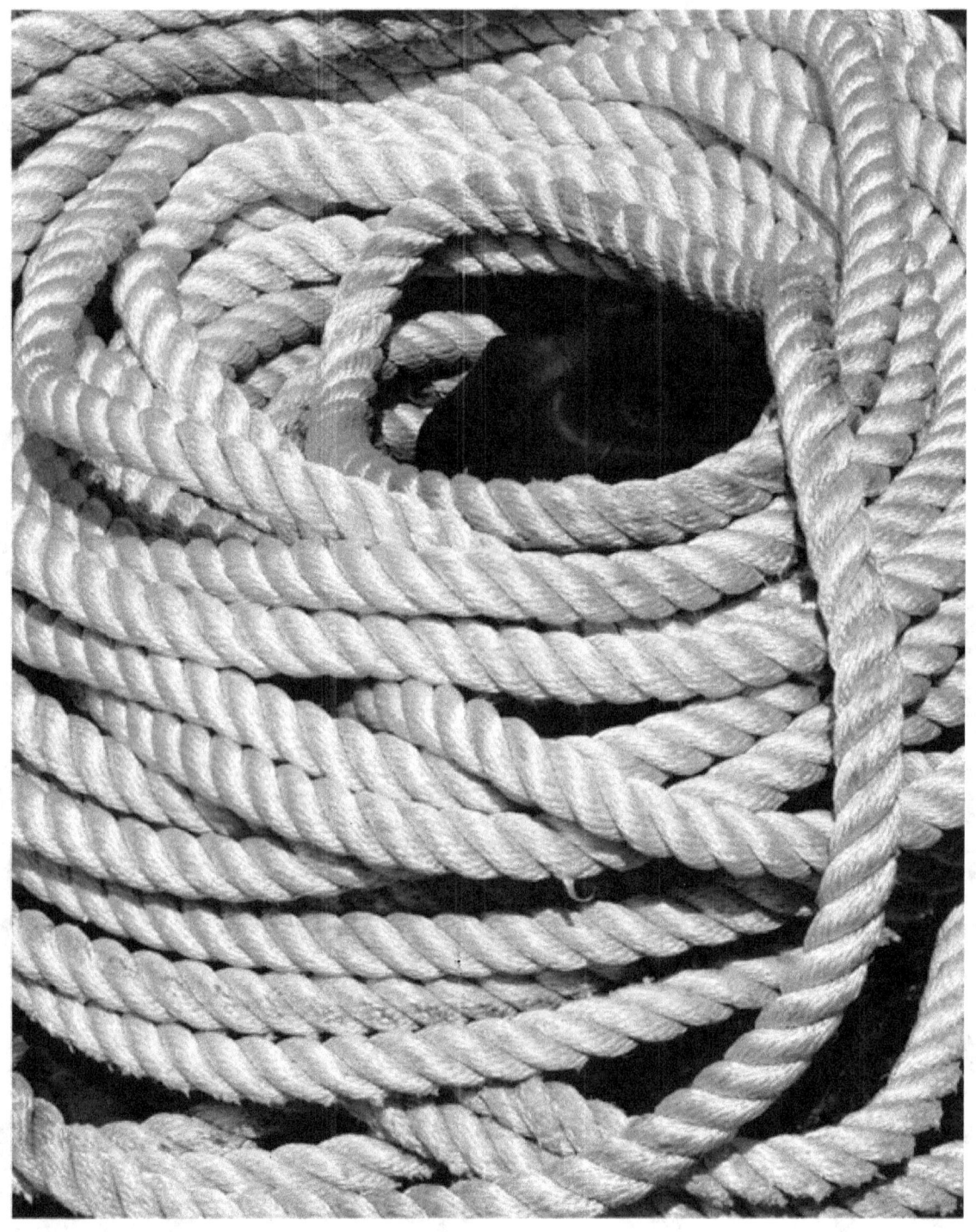

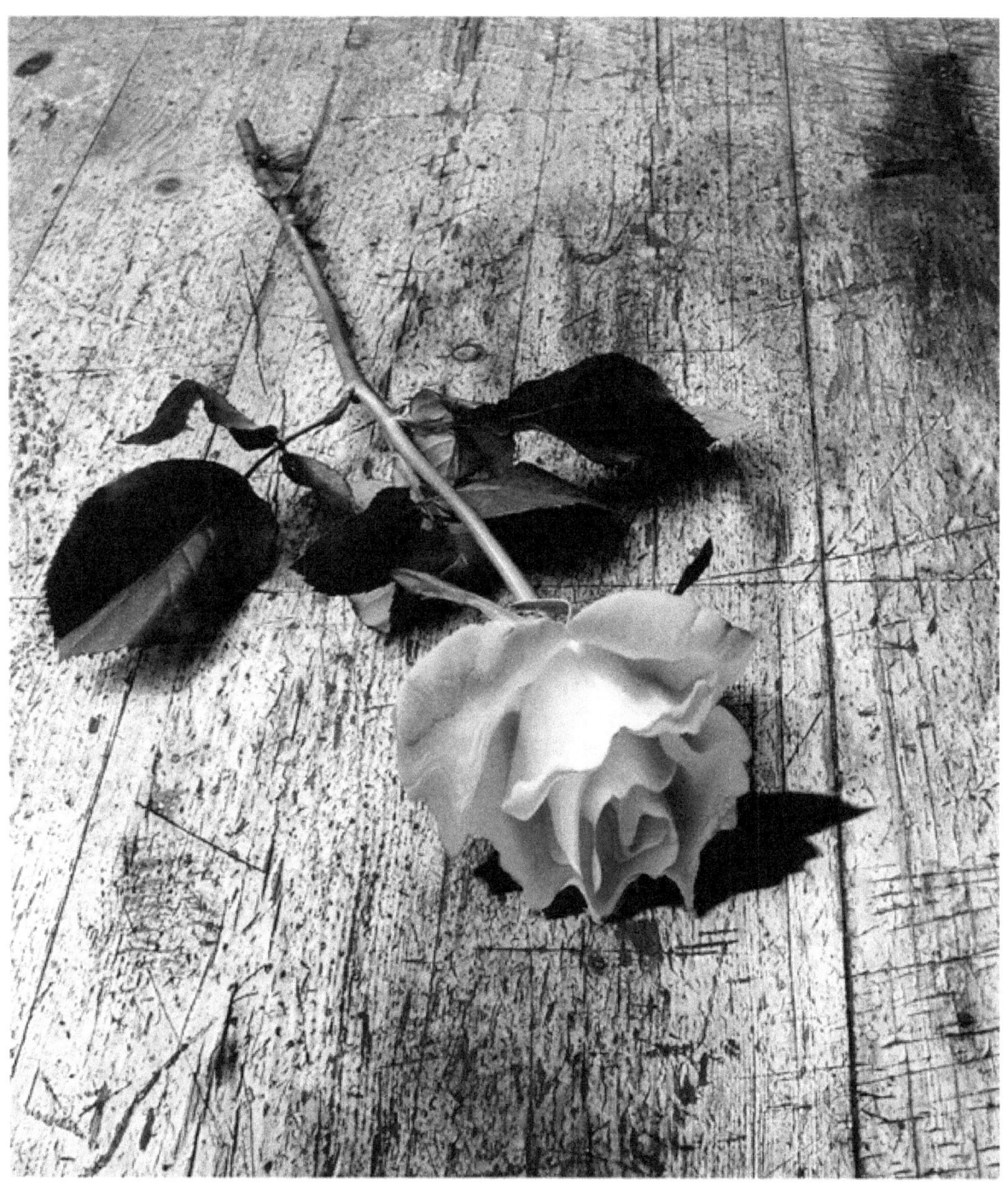

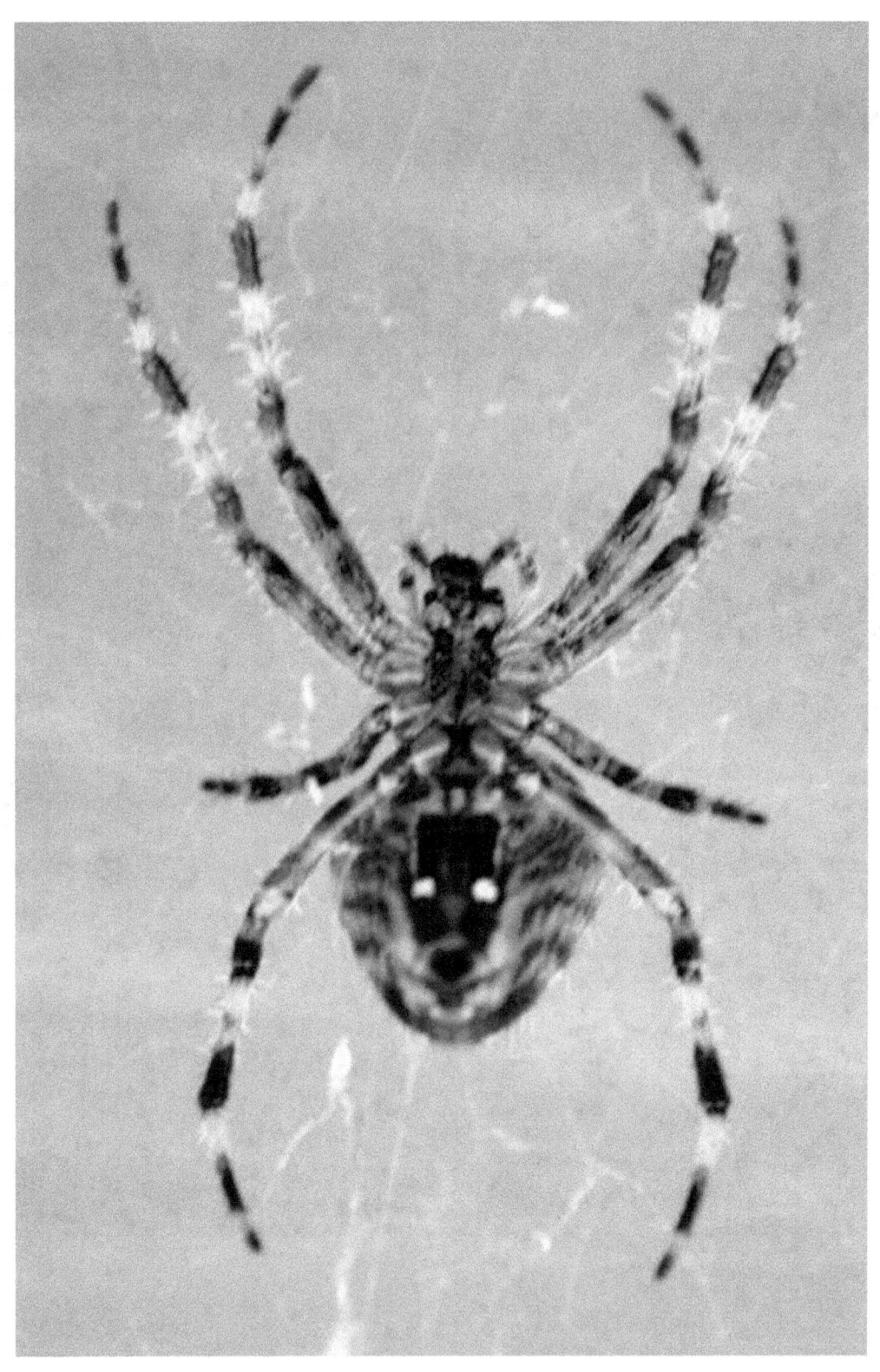

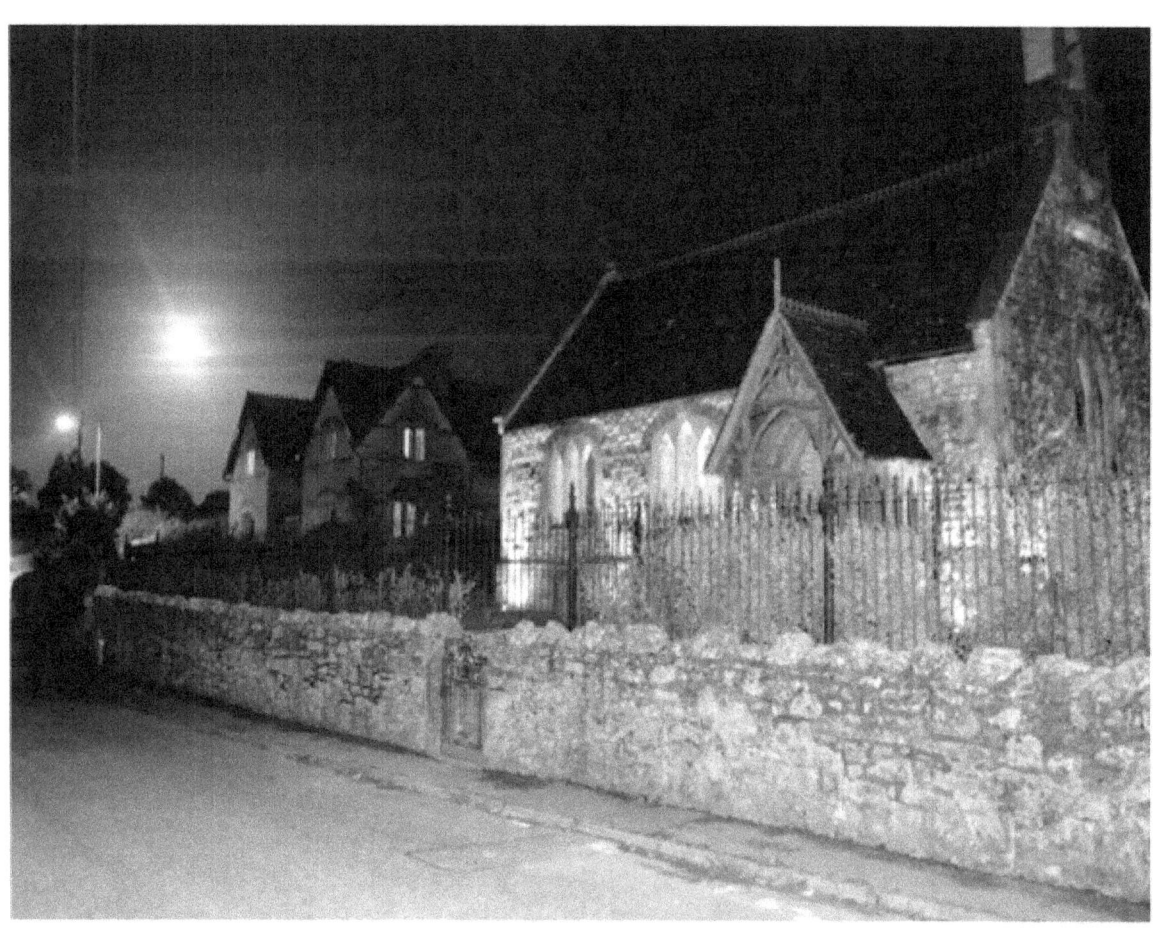

INDEX OF IMAGES

www.ingramcontent.com/pod-product-compliance
Lightning Source LLC
Chambersburg PA
CBHW081742220526
45468CB00008B/2201